ETHICAL OPPORTUNITY COST:

It's a matter of choice

Dr. S. L. Young

Dedications

<u>To my mom:</u> Thank you for teaching me the difference between "right and wrong" and "good and bad," while also stressing that I must be accountable and responsible for my choices. You instilled in me the confidence to not blindly follow others, which may lead me to a place that I might not want to go.

<u>To those who face unethical challenges:</u> Ethical dilemmas are encountered in many organizations. However, you don't need to be a party (willing or not) to any unethical activities. Everyone is accountable and responsible for their own actions and behaviors. Furthermore, individuals shouldn't become complicit or culpable to ethical violations by making a choice (active or passive) to allow unethical activities to go unchallenged.

Special thanks to the following for their time and generous support: Virginia Clay, Glenda Coefield, Gina Dunham, Clifton "CJ" Frank, Kimberly Finn, Lisa Fox, Samuel G. Gatling, Patricia Colburn Grossman, Gary Jackson, C. Anthony Lawry, Brian Marhefsky, Carrie Markels, Rokib Masud, Karin Mustoe, Tish Rodgers, Prince Sakyi, Randy Smith, Sr., Virginia Smith, Scotia Wade, Gioia Yvonne Wallace, and Joanne Workman

Table of Contents

Foreword 1

Preface..4

<u>Chapter 1:</u> Ethics – What Is It? 6

<u>Chapter 2:</u> Honesty – The Best Policy 9

<u>Chapter 3:</u> Ethical Activities Illustrated.....................12

<u>Chapter 4:</u> Factors That Influence Someone's Ethics 17

<u>Chapter 5:</u> Character Versus Ethics............................21

<u>Chapter 6:</u> Ethical Opportunity Cost 26

<u>Chapter 7:</u> Types of Ethical Violations.......................30

<u>Chapter 8:</u> Ethics: More Than a Concept, Consideration, or Convenience..33

<u>Chapter 9:</u> Reasons Individuals Choose to Be Unethical 36

<u>Chapter 10:</u> Good Actions Can Lead to a Bad Outcome 39

<u>Chapter 11:</u> Submitting Incorrect Customer Data.................44

<u>Chapter 12:</u> Money Transferred to Unauthorized Accounts 48

<u>Chapter 13:</u> Ordering Equipment and Services Before It's Needed..52

<u>Chapter 14:</u> Hiring Relatives or Friends Without the Required Skills..57

<u>Chapter 15:</u> Using Past Working Dinners to Influence Future Actions 62

Chapter 16: Disparate Treatment................................66

Chapter 17: Receiving Credit That Isn't Due 72

Chapter 18: Accepting Loan Data Without Verifiable
Applicant Information..76

Chapter 19: Changing Audit Results to Meet a Client's
Needs 80

Chapter 20: Questionable Business Practices.....................88

Chapter 21: Every Student Receives a Perfect Grade 95

Chapter 22: Stop the Timer..100

Chapter 23: Workplace Abuse.....................................105

Chapter 24: An Unnecessary Verbal Attack.......................111

Chapter 25: Academic Dishonesty.................................116

Chapter 26: Company Responsibility 123

Chapter 27: Individual Responsibility 126

Chapter 28: Ethical Violations Impact on Others 129

Chapter 29: Ethical Violations Statistics 133

Chapter 30: Underreporting of Ethical Violations 136

Chapter 31: Costs of Not Reporting Unethical Activities ...139

Chapter 32: Helping the Ethically Challenged 142

Chapter 33: Parting Thoughts 144

Appendix A: Ethical Behavior – Individual Responsibility
....152

Appendix B: Are You Really Committed to Your Beliefs? ....
....157

Appendix C: Belief – An Underutilized Tool.......................161

Appendix D: Are You Really Who You Think You Are?..........
....166

Appendix E: What If?! 171

Appendix F: Confronted with an Ethical Dilemma: What
Will You Do?..177

Appendix G: Ethical Training Is Missing the Mark: Here's
Why 182

Appendix H: High School Friends, Different Ethical Paths,
Almost Identical Tragic Endings 187

Appendix I: Becoming a Better Man 193

Figures 200

References 201

About the Author...203

Foreword

There are numerous news reports about individuals who choose to engage in unethical activities. However, these reports don't begin to address the countless number of individuals who engage in unethical activities and don't get caught. Regardless of whether unethical individuals are caught or not, there should be significant concerns about a growing culture that's focused on a "win or succeed" at any cost mentality.

As a college professor, the importance of ethics and ethical actions and/or behaviors[1] is discussed in all my classes. One day while covering a class for another professor, I facilitated a discussion about ethics. During this discussion, the students were given a scenario about an employee who chose to not engage in an unethical and maybe illegal activity.

The details of this scenario were that an employee decided to not change audit results to meet a client's political and funding needs. After a consultation with the executive team, the executives supported the employee's position until the client threatened future business opportunities if the changes weren't made as requested.

After the client's demands and threats, the executive team directed the employee to make the questionable and maybe illegal changes to maintain a significant revenue contributor for the company.

The students were then asked, "What would you do as the

---

[1] Action(s) and/or behavior(s) are most times referred to in this book as an "activity" or "activities."

employee if your employer directed you to make changes to an independent audit report that would manipulate the results to no longer reflect your findings"? The students' responses were surprising.

Over 75% of the class said that the questionable and potentially illegal changes should be made as the executives and client instructed.

The students were then asked about the reasons that the executives' directions would be followed. Most of the students' responses were either: "I have to follow all of my executives' instructions" or "I wouldn't want to do it, but I would do it because I don't want to lose my job."

The correct answer is that employees don't have to engage in questionable, unethical, or illegal activity regardless of the source of the direction.

Individuals will sometimes not want to comply with a leader's direction. However, at times, individuals will have an internal conflict that may cause a normally trustworthy person to act inappropriately. This type of internal conflict can be driven by a fear of losing a job, a lack of understanding about someone's rights, respect for an authority figure, someone's position, or other factors.

It's important to note that it can also be difficult for individuals to behave ethically for various reasons. Although, choosing to act or behave unethically due to fear isn't an acceptable alternative either.

Someone's actions and activities (ethical or not) reflect their character, which won't vary that often based on the situation. At times, it can be challenging to act and/or behave ethically, but the long-term cost(s) to individuals, companies, or societies for unethically activities can be much costlier for individuals and organizations due to lost revenues, damaged reputations, ill-gotten gains, and more.

Given a choice as to whether to act and/or behave ethically or not… what will you choose?

Preface

In many of my undergraduate and graduate business classes, there were often discussions about the importance of being ethical. Most of these classes focused on someone's responsibility to not engage in illicit, illegal, or questionable activities. However, none of these discussions addressed the potential issues that can emerge because someone willingly chooses to not be complicit (by allowing unethical activities to continue unquestioned or unchallenged).

Ethical conduct can be based on culture, family values, training, religion, beliefs, or other considerations. Any of these factors can influence someone's ethical activities. Although, ultimately the responsibility to behave ethically and to report unethical activities is everyone's responsibility[2].

It's understood that it can be a tough decision to choose to get involved with or report unethical activities.

Some of the reasons that individuals choose to not get involved after the discovery of unethical activities are the fear of retaliation, being identified as a troublemaker, the loss of a job, the risk of losing friends/associates, etc. Independently each of these reasons can be very powerful motivators for individuals to not report unethical activities.

This leads to the question: "Should someone be responsible for the outcome of any unethical actions, behaviors, or the subsequent outcome(s) if the discovered activities aren't

---

[2] Reference the article "High School Friends, Different Ethical Paths, Almost Identical Tragic Endings" in Appendix H.

reported?" There isn't an easy answer to this question. However, the part that's easy to resolve is that unethical activity shouldn't go unreported, unchallenged, or uncontrolled… whether it's reported directly or indirectly.

This book uses case studies to review and conduct analysis of unethical activities that were primarily encountered during my professional career. The goal of this material isn't to provide an absolute guide on ways to deal with unethical activities. Although, this book can be a tool to determine actionable options if unethical activities are encountered.

Ultimately, everyone is responsible and accountable for ethical activities, compliance, reporting, and prevention. Therefore, it's important to ask the question:

If unethical activities are encountered, what will <u>you choose</u> to do[3]?

_____

[3] Reference the article "Becoming A Better Man" in Appendix I.

Chapter 1:

Ethics – What Is It?

Many individuals if asked, "What are ethics?" will either say, "It's doing the right thing;" "It's good or bad;" "It's right or wrong." These answers aren't incorrect, but only reflect just a portion of the components of ethics.

Ethical activities include the definition of ethics, along with an understanding about the importance and impact of someone's ethical actions, behaviors, choices, and decisions.

Components of ethics:

- Ethics – an understanding and application of whether something is good/bad or right/wrong, including an examination as to whether these action(s), behavior(s), choice(s), and/or decision(s) are appropriate

  o Ethical behavior can be influenced based on someone's education, experiences, environments, expectations, or external factors. Also, activities (intentional or unintentional) can reflect these considerations and oftentimes the belief(s) of an individual, a group, or an organization

- Ethical Activities – things done that are open, honest, and with integrity, along with not being purposefully deceptive or with an intent to defraud

- Ethical Decision-Making – a process used to make a choice or decision that's truthful, done in good faith, and isn't intended to be deceptive, fraudulent, or do harm

- Ethical Decision – a thoughtful and just outcome after an ethical determination based on ethical decision making

Each of these components is involved in the consideration of ethics, being ethical, and making ethical decisions.

Ethical decisions should be made without consideration(s) about the outcome. This, at times, can lead to very tough decisions. However, ethical decisions shouldn't be made based on the potential consequences. These types of decisions should instead be made based on a desire to engage in ethical activities.

Ethical individuals shouldn't focus on asking themselves "Will there be consequences for my action(s) or behavior(s)?" because their decisions should be based on the consideration and not the outcome. Notwithstanding, there should be an evaluation about the potential impacts of their decision(s), along with a determination about ways to minimize them through risk mitigation activities.

Considerations for ethical decision-making:

1. Honest – Is there a desire to reveal all available information?

2. Truthful – Is there an intent to deceive or defraud?

3. Compliant – Are activities within legal, policy, or procedural guidelines?

4. Responsible – Are activities unnecessarily impactful to others (e.g., individuals, organizations, society)?

By making judgments based on these questions, individuals will more likely make better decisions that are consistent with ethical standards, actions, and/or behaviors that are beneficial to society.

Chapter 2:

Honesty – The Best Policy

Many individuals have heard the phrase, "Honesty is the best policy," but what does this really mean?

- Should individuals take a literal meaning to the phrase and no matter the situation or circumstance tell the (sometimes hurtful) truth?

- Could there be exceptions to this expression?

- Should there be consideration(s) given while deciding whether to apply this guidance?

Generally, honesty is the best policy!

Notwithstanding, there are times that honest and accurate information must be conveyed in a manner that protects individuals, organizations, or companies from unnecessarily hurtful communication. During these times, individuals have a responsibility to be truthful but should approach their communication, action(s), or behavior(s) in a manner that doesn't unnecessarily hurt, intimidate, demean, insult, or otherwise intentionally abuse others.

Individuals should be mindful that there will be times that honest and ethical concerns won't be wanted or desired, which could be due to management's direction, political motivations, desires to withhold information, or other reasons. Therefore, individuals who report unethical activities must be prepared for negative backlash due to any disclosures.

Any backlash received might be challenging to deal with initially. However, the backlash will be much less impactful (individually or professionally) than someone who becomes complicit by not addressing or allowing the unethical activities to continue.

While making ethical choices and decisions, "Honesty is the best policy." Moreover, information should be provided or presented in a manner that doesn't make anyone feel less than their perceived worth (even though others might not be supportive about any disclosures related to potentially unethical activities).

Chapter 3:

Ethical Activities Illustrated

Being ethical isn't a point on a chart or a timeline nor is it a destination. Moreover, *"Ethical behavior is pretty clear; the part that's gray is individual interpretation.[4]"*

Ethical activities are part of a continuum that can be viewed differently depending on the moment reviewed or the collective composite of someone's experiences over time. For example, a decision made early in someone's career or life might be viewed as ethical. However, years later the earlier decision might be considered differently (questionable or unethical) with the benefit of time, distance, and experience.

Ethical activities begin with an individual, but are driven by a collection of individual experiences/associations with family, friends, colleagues, educators, managers, etc. Although, the determination of whether an action and/or behavior is ethical is usually an individual experience and choice.

An illustration may be useful.

If ethics is viewed as an illustration with ethical activities represented above the line and unethical activities represented below the line, point A (Figure 1.0) is the baseline for expected ethical activities.

It's important to note that there are varying degrees to someone's ethical or unethical activities. Point A merely represents a starting point, as someone's activities can be further categorized depending on the severity of their activities.

---

[4] Young, S. L. It's a Crazy World…Learn From It: Part II – Moving Forward. Arlington, Virginia: Beyond SPRH, LLC, 2012 - 2014, 2023 - 2024, p. 34. Print.

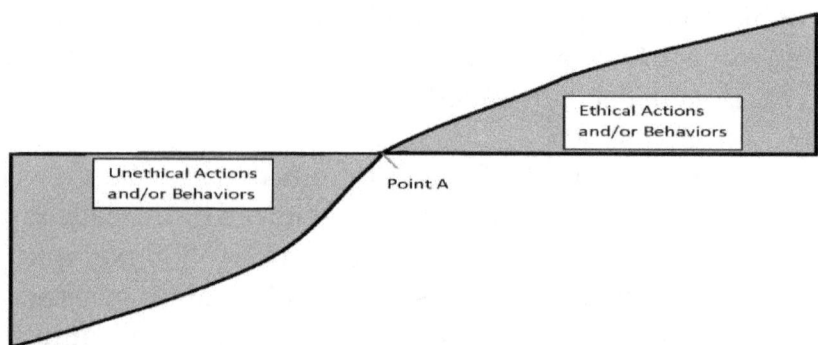

Figure 1.0: Baseline Representation of Ethical Behavior

For example, let's imagine that a cashier takes money from a cash register. This cashier (to minimize questions about missing funds) decides to only take pennies from the drawer. The manager notices that the drawer is short by small amounts every day but doesn't inquire about the shortages and doesn't take any corrective action. Therefore, the cashier continues to take pennies for a while, which slowly become dollars.

The cashier's ethical baseline (and considerations about their ethical activities) shifts to point B (Figure 1.1).

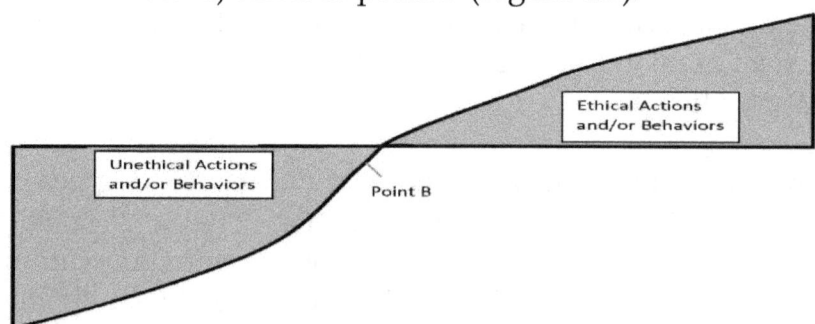

Figure 1.1: Cashier's Initial Ethical Baseline

Since the manager didn't take any corrective action about the minimal amounts of missing cash each day, the cashier decided that there aren't any concerns with the daily drawer shortages. At this point, the cashier begins to take nickels. Now, the amount of money stolen by the cashier grows at a faster rate.

The cashier's ethical baseline (and considerations about their ethical activities) shifts again. This time the cashier's baseline moves to point C (Figure 1.2).

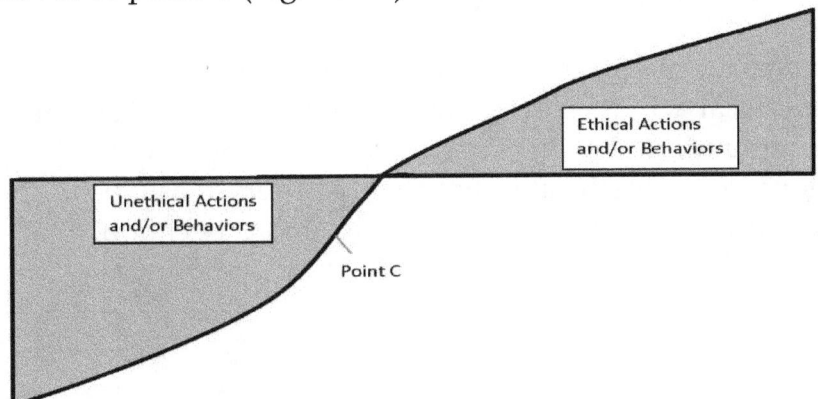

Figure 1.2: Cashier's Decreasing Ethical Baseline

Every time someone makes a choice to be unethical, their decision has the potential to shift their ethical baseline from point A (Figure 1.0) to a new location depending on their choice(s), subsequent decisions, activities, and behaviors.

Someone's ethical baseline can quickly change depending on the severity of their activities. Therefore, each time someone faces an ethical consideration or dilemma, there is a potential to adjust their starting point for ethical activities to move further from or closer to point A.

The further someone moves below the ethical baseline at point A and downward, the more difficult it will be to return to the minimum starting point for expected ethical activities without corrective action.

This realization supports the need for adequate controls to be implemented to prevent, discourage, or resolve any ethical issues as soon as possible. By addressing questionable or unethical issues quickly, there are less opportunities or reasons for ethical violations to continue.

An important message communicated by a timely response to any unethical activities is that ethical violations aren't wanted, are monitored, and will be dealt with swiftly. By resolving questionable or unethical issues timely, it serves as a powerful tool for ethical compliance, monitoring, and prevention.

Chapter 4:

Factors That Influence Someone's Ethics

Individuals choose to be unethical for various reasons, such as greed, bad decisions, peer-pressure, etc. However, one of the biggest factors that influences someone's ethical decisions is the presence of an opportunity. Therefore, organizations must prioritize the implementation of systematic processes and controls.

Organizations that implement barriers to opportunities for unethical activities help to reduce incidents of improper behavior.

The removal of opportunity is an important deterrent, because individuals who experience significant barriers to unethical activities will usually reconsider their activities (especially if there's an increased probability of being caught).

Factors that influence someone's ethical activities:

- Choices – bad choices are made with or without consideration(s) about the correctness, fairness, morality, or humanity of the activities

- Consistency – the lack of equality in the application or enforcement of policies and procedures can lead individuals to engage in inappropriate activities if there's a reduced possibility to get caught

- Controls – insufficient controls to monitor, identify, report, and control unethical activities

- Enforcement – the lack of any or visible consequences to address unethical violations can lead to orchestrated and systematic abuses

- <u>Family and Friends</u> – members of a social circle can have a significant influence on someone's decision-making process(es), because oftentimes individuals will emulate the activities of those who the individual has close relationships, values, or trusts

- <u>Fear</u> – a concern about rejection or being thought of badly if someone doesn't behave similarly

- <u>Laws</u> – enacted legislation with penalties (e.g., jail time, financial consequences) for infractions can be a strong motivator for individuals to not engage in illegal or unethical activities

- <u>Leadership</u> – an organization's leaders' activities are important because employees will often emulate the activities exhibited by management

- <u>Morals</u> –personal beliefs can be a significant factor in determining whether activities are ethical

- <u>Opportunity</u> – an absence of implemented policies, procedures, and audits may lead to increased incidents of unethical activities

- <u>Peer Pressure</u> – individuals are sometimes influenced by the actions of others instead of using their own judgment to make the most appropriate decision

- <u>Retaliation</u> – individuals sometimes follow others out of concern or fear that there might be backlash if unethical activities aren't followed, supported, or are reported

- <u>Policy and Procedures</u> – documented behavioral rules and guidelines should be created to ensure that everyone clearly understands about expectations for acceptable activities

This is a partial list of reasons that might affect someone's decision(s) whether to engage in unethical activities. However, one of these factors is important enough to highlight separately, which is the "power of choice" ... because (many times) individuals have an option to select between one decision versus another.

Individuals should be held responsible and accountable for their activities. Although, it's understood that there might be times that someone might not be fully accountable for their actions (e.g., mental capacity, fear of their life). Nevertheless, these examples are extreme and don't occur often.

A determination as to whether someone is ethical or not is a personal choice. Furthermore, the decisions someone makes despite opportunities to do otherwise separates those who have a higher ethical standard from those who do not.

It might be difficult to engage in appropriate ethical activities all the time, but there are seldom any justifiable reasons to act and/or behave unethically.

Chapter 5:

Character Versus Ethics

Ethical training normally focuses on "good versus bad" and "right versus wrong" activities, along with any other standards (e.g., policies, procedures, customs) that must be followed. Also, during this type of training, there are usually discussions about someone's responsibility and accountability to make ethical decisions (even if there's an opportunity to do otherwise).

Organizational policies and procedures provide guidance, reinforce, and sometimes build on the lessons individuals learn throughout their life. As part of an organization's indoctrination, it must ensure that its members are educated about standards, understand the potential consequences of unacceptable behavior, and are informed about the penalties for non-compliance. Therefore, ethical training is an important process and procedural step to ensure that organizational members are taught about its culture (e.g., beliefs, attitudes, values), including its ethical standards.

Organizational character is just a part of ethical behavior and conformance (although a significant portion). Another valuable consideration is related to individual character, which is very important since an organization's character is based on the collective actions of various contributors.

Individual character[5] is developed over a lifetime. During this time, individuals explore concepts and considerations about whether something is "good or bad" or "right or wrong." This, however, isn't the only part of the ethical decision-making process. Individual character is rather complicated because it reflects someone's attitudes, beliefs, considerations, choices,

---

[5] Reference the article "Ethical Behavior – Individual Responsibility" in Appendix A.

and much more.

During an onboarding process, individuals are usually taught about processes that can be used to make ethical decisions within an organization. Although, even after being educated about an organization's ethical standards, ethical decisions are ultimately an individual responsibility to choose to "do the right thing" despite any opportunities to engage in unethical activities.

While making an ethical decision, individuals use a variety of life experiences and beliefs to reach their viewpoint(s).

Components of someone's ethical decisions:

- Beliefs – personal views about an action or behavior

- Culture – value system of an environment

- Expectations – communicated guidelines about the way ethical dilemmas should be handled

- Management – direction of formal and informal expectations for organizational compliance

- Morals – core belief system that drives someone's response to certain activities

- Experiences – lessons learned from previous events/circumstances

- Peer Pressure – influence by others to act or behave a certain manner

- Role Model – someone who is used as a behavioral or informational reference point to determine appropriate activities/behaviors

- Values – things that align with someone's core beliefs

These components (and others) influence someone's character.

Character is one of the most important factors in making ethical choices or decisions because someone's activities reflect their motives.

Taking it a little further…

Ethics is ultimately a process to determine if something is "right or "wrong." Ethical activities are driven by someone's core beliefs, family, society, education, opportunity, relationships (personal/business), life challenges, and more.

Ethics generally provides a baseline to determine whether something is an appropriate action or behavior, but it doesn't always take into consideration personal beliefs. The reason that personal beliefs are important is that someone's beliefs might not align with the environmental factors related to the organization that someone belongs.

Character is displayed through someone's actions, behaviors, and choices. Character also, generally, reflects someone's core beliefs that are often engaged while making decisions.

Whenever someone is presented with a choice, personal character affects the way in which a situation is handled that goes beyond a determination as to whether something is "right or wrong" or "good or bad." A choice might be considered "right or good" based on professional or societal standards but might still be "wrong or bad" based on someone's personal belief(s). Character is something that exists over and above others' considerations of and about ethical behavior. Character reflects someone's true nature. It also defines someone's core beliefs in terms of whether values will be compromised to achieve an end-result.

Anyone who only considers the ethical impact(s) of their activities may rationalize their activities as a social or societal norm to conform. Conversely, someone with a high character standard won't do something just because it conforms with social/societal norms or peer pressure. Instead, this person will base their choices on various factors, but their decisions will be highly influenced based on their core values, belief system, hopefully a desire to "do the right thing" … regardless of the potential consequences.

Ethics provide guidelines for "good versus bad" or "right versus wrong" behavior. However, it's individual character (including core values) that defines the things that someone will do even if the ethical litmus test on the surface indicates that the choice(s) made is acceptable.

Ultimately, it's individual character that's used to examine the situation a step further to determine whether a decision fits within someone's core beliefs and values.

This last consideration defines individual character, which isn't dependent on a situation.

Chapter 6:

Ethical Opportunity Cost

Individual activities are important factors in ethical actions behaviors, and compliance. However, significant factors in ethical activities are related to ethical opportunity cost.

Opportunity cost is a mindful decision to do activity X instead of Y, which represents a trade-off of doing one thing versus another. As a result, someone's time, energy, and effort that's directed toward activity X detracts from their ability to pursue activity Y. Moreover, additional focus will be directed toward activity X because it's perceived to have or will create greater value (e.g., personal, professional, financial).

As it relates to ethical activities, there can be unintended consequences for someone's (and others) actions taken or behaviors performed to meet or exceed ethical expectations. The reason that ethical opportunity costs are significant is that everyone doesn't agree that or want ethical activities to be enforced, which can be a pivotal issue with ethical actions, behaviors, compliance, and decisions.

The ongoing challenge during many ethical training sessions is that many times it's used to define ethics, discuss acceptable behavioral standards, perform ethical exercises, and detail the consequences of not acting or behaving ethically. Notwithstanding, these sessions would also benefit from allowing additional time to detail the reasons that someone's willingness to question and/or report unethical activities is a crucial factor in maintaining an organizational culture that's based on ethics, integrity, and trust.

Many ethical training sessions (seldom if ever) include discussions about the potential personal consequences (e.g., retaliation, backlash, isolation) of following the training's guidance to remedy, report, or resolve ethical dilemmas. This is something that needs to change and be included in all ethical training discussions.

The personal, negative consequences of being an ethical person include:

- Backlash – negative consequences for acting/behaving a certain way

- Isolation – community or organizational members stop or limit their interactions with someone

- Labeled – derogatory terms/references are directed at or associated with someone who questions or combats unwanted activities

- Retaliation – actions purposely taken against someone as a payback for past and unwelcome activities.

There can also be unintended consequences directed toward individuals who act or behave ethically so that others:

- Don't want to get involved

- Don't provide support to resolve the issue(s)

- Create obstacles to resolve any investigations

- Harass, intimidate, or threaten individuals who want to act and/or behave ethically

- Aren't involved with an issue or investigation and inappropriately insert themselves into the situation

These types of unintended, negative consequences aren't often discussed but should be a part of ethical training to prepare individuals for the unexpected potential outcome(s) related to attempts to act and/or behave ethically.

It's important to note that it won't always be easy to act and/or behave ethically. However, the choice(s) someone makes to engage in ethical activities is better than choosing to ignore or not prevent unethical ones, including being complicit to unethical activities by not reporting (even anonymously) questionable or unethical behavior in a timely manner.

Chapter 7:

Types of Ethical Violations

Ethical beliefs (for the most part) are developed based on various factors: family/friends, religion, experiences, training, and other factors.

<u>Ethical violations are caused by these factors or beliefs:</u>

- <u>Character</u> – a personal belief system, which drives someone to respond a certain way, even though others might behave differently

- <u>Cultural</u> – the immediate living or social environment influences someone's belief system

- <u>Illegal</u> – anything that isn't lawful

- <u>Intentional</u> – something that's knowingly done that isn't compliant with acceptable standards of behavior related to cultural, organizational, personal, or societal standards about "right or wrong" or "good or bad"

- <u>Moral</u> – activities done that aren't aligned with someone's core beliefs, along with not being connected to their attitude about being righteous, socially aware, or attempting to benefit the greater good

- <u>Organizational</u> – inconsistent activities that differ from an organization's determinations about appropriate or permissible activities

- <u>Relational</u> – negative or questionable individuals who challenge someone to act or behave negatively based on their associations within a circle-of-influence

- <u>Societal</u> – customary activities that are considered "right or wrong" or "good or bad" within a specific population

- <u>Unintentional</u> – activities that aren't intended to be unethical

There are different types of ethical violations that are acceptable in some environments and under certain circumstances. However, many times, these violations aren't allowed due to permissive standards within associations, groups, and/or organizations. Notwithstanding, policies and procedures must be comprehensive to address various ethical violation scenarios to be fully effective. This focus also strengthens other ethical initiatives (e.g., operating guidelines, training).

Chapter 8:

Ethics: More Than a Concept, Consideration, or Convenience

Ethical activities are based on choices, but began with an understanding, evaluation, and application of the word "ethics." A customary definition of ethics is related to things that are "good or bad" or "right or wrong." This is a start; however, it's only the beginning.

For someone to make a choice as to whether activities are ethical, there must be a consideration about the components of ethical beliefs:

- Concept – Is this considered to be true?

- Consideration – Is this true for me?

- Convenience – Is this true for me at this moment?

Individuals must also evaluate these tenets that underline the basis for ethical decision-making:

- Concept – Is this something that's generally accepted to be true and will be applied?

- Consideration – Is this something that there's a possibility to act or behave a certain way (there might or might not be a willingness to act)?

- Convenience – Is this something that will only be done if it meets an objective (personal or otherwise)?

Someone might believe that ethical beliefs (as a concept) are true. If so, then there should be a demonstration of this belief in their activities. Although, at times, individuals in choosing their activities will consider other factors, such as whether the concept applies to themselves or the situation. However, oftentimes, activities aren't based on ethical concepts or considerations, but instead primarily on personal convenience for themselves... and sometimes others.

Individuals might be more willing to disregard their so-called belief(s) (temporarily or permanently), which don't align with their (current or future) wants, needs, or desires. This consideration is especially true for any situation that may lead to an opportunity for personal benefit (e.g., financial gain, organizational standing, academic achievement).

Notwithstanding earlier commentary, anyone who is firm in their core beliefs (e.g., morals, values, attitudes) won't easily disregard these important considerations for the sake of temporary convenience, including opportunities for short-term gains.

Therefore, if someone can easily disregard their core beliefs based on convenience, what does this imply or convey about their "strength-of-character?" This rhetorical question is not for me to answer but is an important consideration.[6]

Reference the article "Are You Really Committed to Your Beliefs?" in Appendix B.

Chapter 9:

Reasons Individuals
Choose to Be Unethical

A decision to be unethical is almost always an individual choice, excluding unintentional activities.

Individuals who choose to be unethical usually do so uncoerced but are sometimes influenced by others who have identified or created an opportunity to be unethical.

Reasons individuals choose to be unethical:

- Advancement – an attempt to obtain a promotional opportunity within an organization

- Follower – decides to engage in unethical activities because others do

- Money - pursuit of financial goals

- Opportunity - absence of controls to prevent or minimize unethical activities

- Pressure – influenced or coerced to participate either willingly or unwillingly

- Recuperation – belief that an outstanding debt is due, or compensation is warranted for past actions, which results in something of value being taken illegally

- Reputation/Status – based on character, actions, or perceptions, it's believed (whether true or not) that someone is above/better than others or the system(s); therefore, these types of individuals are allowed to manipulate or leverage connections to outsmart controls (e.g., system, processes)

- <u>Retaliation</u> – a negative repayment or attacks for past activities or perceived wrongs

- <u>Sampling</u> - testing controls (e.g., systems, processes) at different times, locations, and various degrees to determine if opportunities exist or can be created to exploit vulnerabilities

- <u>Superstar</u> - a belief that there won't be consequences for someone's activities based on an internal belief that the person is too good or important to be held accountable or responsible

Individuals who choose to be unethical must be prepared to receive any consequences for their actions (whether the person willingly or unwillingly decides to participate).

Chapter 10:

Good Actions Can
Lead to a Bad Outcome

My earliest memory about dealing with an ethical dilemma was in junior high school. This was the first time that I learned from direct experience that attempting to "do the right thing" could lead to a negative outcome.

In junior high, there was a young lady I liked (let's call her "Jenny") who was very pretty, outgoing, and had a great personality. These traits made me like Jenny more and more each day until an unexpected event occurred.

One day, Jenny and I were having lunch. We were having a good time as normal until Jenny showed and offered me some black pills, which I would later discover to be "speed." I was very disappointed that Jenny had and wanted to use drugs. Up until this point, I thought that Jenny had it all and was someone who I wanted to spend more time hanging-out.

After Jenny gave me the pills to examine, I refused to give them back to her. My refusal led to a big fight.

The next day shortly after returning to school, I was directed to go to the principal's office. While walking to the principal's office, I didn't understand the reason for my visit. However, it wouldn't take long for me to discover the reason for my visit. Upon my arrival, the principal questioned me about the pills that were taken from Jenny.

I admitted that I had the pills the previous day but didn't tell the principal that the pills were taken from Jenny to prevent her from taking them. Also, I didn't disclose that the pills weren't for me, as I didn't want or take them. Nevertheless, my punishment was a five day out-of-school suspension.

You might wonder about the way the principal discovered that I had the pills the previous day. I never received a definitive answer about the source of the principal's knowledge, but I had my suspicions. The interesting thing is that the only individual who knew that I kept the pills was Jenny, unless someone overheard our loud discussion in the cafeteria or witnessed the pill exchange.

Regardless of the situation, I didn't have the pills on my me the day I was suspended from school for drug possession. Nevertheless, the worse part was that I was suspended for doing the "right thing," and Jenny who brought the drugs to school wasn't punished for doing the "wrong thing." Notwithstanding, I accepted responsibility for my suspension because I had a false sense of loyalty to someone who in hindsight didn't deserve it.

This was the first time that there was a realization that good behavior wouldn't always be rewarded and could also lead to negative outcomes, but this wouldn't be the last painful example.

Questions

1) If a friend was about to take drugs, would you do anything to prevent it? Why or why not?

2) Would you return pills to a friend that were given to you to examine? Why or why not?

3) Would you have told the principal who gave you the pills? Why or why not?

4) Would you ask the individual who gave you the pills about the source of the principal's knowledge? Why or why not?

5) Would you remain friends with the individual who originally had the drugs if you were suspended for drug possession? Why or why not?

Lessons Learned

Behaving ethically won't always lead to an expected result, but it's still the "right thing" to do. As sometimes, someone might not be able to control others' activities after discovering and/or evaluating behavior or situations. Nevertheless, it's always better to do the "right thing" versus living with yourself for doing something wrong.

It can be a difficult choice to decide to address questionable activities. Although it can be a tougher decision to allow a questionable activity to knowingly occur, not take corrective action, and later discover that someone's lack of involvement led to a bad outcome for others.

The other important considerations from this case are: How far might you be willing to be punished to protect a friend? Is it ever acceptable to plead "guilty" for an activity that you didn't do?

Unethical Activity Types:
- Character
- Illegal
- Relational
- Societal

Chapter 11:

Submitting Incorrect

Customer Data

As a billing representative, a large portion of the job involved answering customer billing inquiries, resolving billing issues, and contacting customers to collect meter readings for unbilled equipment.

The process used to call (sometimes hundreds of) customers was a challenging task. It wasn't because collecting meter readings was a difficult or exciting activity. At times, it could take several phone calls, many days, and speaking to multiple contacts to obtain the required information.

The rush to collect billable information was always hectic near the end of the billing period, as the team worked to maximize the percentage of successfully billed equipment. This stress was heightened due to a collective desire to achieve the highest percentage of billed equipment, which also prevented a negative impact on the team's performance objectives.

Any equipment that wasn't billed could potentially cause a representative to miss their performance objectives. For this reason, some of the billing representatives would create an estimated meter reading. Then, this falsified information would be entered into the system to bill the equipment, which also resulted in a lower unbilled percentage.

This practice of submitting estimated meter reading wasn't permitted. However, some billing representatives openly discussed the practice. This behavior didn't appear to be a habitual team effort. Although, some representatives would do whatever was needed to meet their billing objectives.

Questions

1) Is it ever acceptable to enter a meter reading that wasn't received from a validated source? If so, why? If not, why not?

2) Might there be a time that an estimated meter reading would be acceptable (even if the practice was against policies and procedures)? If so, when might this be acceptable? If not, why not?

3) Would you be tempted to enter an estimated meter reading if it was believed that the practice would most likely not be discovered unless the customer reported it? Why or why not?

4) What type of controls could be created to validate that the meter readings received were accurate?

5) What should happen to a billing representative who uses estimated meter readings that weren't validated on their billing assignment?

Lessons Learned

Everyone won't always follow policies, procedures, or processes as expected. Sometimes individuals will inappropriately leverage their experiential knowledge about organizational, systems', policies', processes', or procedures' weaknesses to (most effectively) meet their needs or achieve their objectives.

Ethical compliance challenges can sometimes be greater if individual's performance reviews are tied to meeting aggressive objectives. This is the reason that process controls and validation points must be used to periodically verify compliance, and to also minimize non-standard behavior that will give anyone an unfair advantage.

Individuals won't always follow the rules or a company's standards (e.g., policies, procedures). Therefore, organizations must "trust but verify" to protect an organization from unnecessary ethical violations that could be minimized or prevented with the implementation of audit controls.

Unethical Activity Types:
- Character
- Intentional
- Organizational

Chapter 12:

Money Transferred to Unauthorized Accounts

One of the challenges in dealing with large account receivables is that there are times that cash receivables are misapplied, or a customer forgets about a credit on file.

Any unapplied cash belongs to the customer regardless of the amount of time held or its value. Therefore, companies have a fiduciary responsibility to protect the customer's assets.

In this organization, a mandatory meeting was held to discuss the cash disbursement process used to issue checks for unclaimed or unapplied payments. This meeting was required because a couple of employees were arrested due to check fraud.

The individuals arrested were accused of changing customer account names and the associated addresses in the system to addresses of their choice. These changes allowed for significant amounts of cash to be embezzled from these customers' accounts and stolen from the company.

After this incident, a procedural change was implemented that required all customer check disbursement requests to be documented, along with having a manager's signature to be processed.

Questions

1) Will the implemented changes prevent this type of fraudulent activity from occurring again? Why or why not?

2) Will the additional scrutiny and increased process controls prevent other types of theft or fraud? Why or why not?

3) Can other type(s) of controls be implemented to prevent fraudulent activities in the future? Why or why not?

4) Why might the suggested controls be important and useful to prevent future activities?

5) Are there other types of changes to consider that are not system or process related that could be implemented? If so, what? If not, why not?

6) What might this incident convey about the necessity to have tighter controls (generally)?

Lessons Learned

Implemented controls won't discover every attempt for someone to be unethical. However, organizations should proactively implement as many controls as possible to minimize opportunities for fraudulent activities.

These types of ethical controls are a deterrent to unethical activities. Also, controls can be used to periodically validate that systems and processes continue to be effective.

Every scenario that someone can create to embezzle funds can't always be protected against. However, organizations must have different validation points to ensure organizational policies are followed and enforced.

Unethical Activity Types:
- Character
- Cultural
- Illegal
- Morals
- Organizational
- Societal

Chapter 13:

Ordering Equipment and Services Before It's Needed

Sometimes companies will do interesting things that make its' members question the reason(s) for the action, behavior, or activity.

This was exact case after a Senior Vice President instructed me to order voicemail equipment (including maintenance agreements) many months before the equipment would be installed or used.

This request was inconsistent with the organizations I had previously worked, which actively worked to minimize cost by delaying equipment or service agreement purchases until absolutely needed. However, in this organization, the direction received was to order all the voicemail systems and maintenance agreements at least 6 - 9 months prior to the first scheduled system installation.

The rationale for this decision was immediately questioned by me (specifically the direction to order and activate maintenance agreements for equipment that wouldn't be installed for many months).

The answer received was unexpected and surprising as the Senior Vice President said to me, "Sometimes we (the company) do stupid things." This response should have been an early indication that something was potentially wrong with the direction received.

My executive's direction was reluctantly followed, and the result was that voice mail systems were purchased and placed in a warehouse without ever being used. Also, the maintenance agreements expired without being utilized.

Questions

1) Is it an employee's responsibility to ensure that company assets are protected? Why or why not?

2) What would you do if your executive directed you to waste company resources (e.g., money, time)?

3) What might be the reason(s) that equipment and maintenance agreements would be purchased but never used?

4) Is it ever justifiable to order equipment or a maintenance agreement without intent to use it? Why or why not?

5) Are there options available for an employee who disagrees with a supervisor's direction? If so, what? If not, why not?

6) Would you have complied with the Senior Vice President's request to knowingly waste company resources? Why or why not?

Lessons Learned

Individuals within companies will sometimes do things that are counter to a company's mission, stated objectives, or best interest.

Direction received from an executive to knowingly waste company resources can be very challenging, along with being difficult to comply with the instructions (especially if someone's personal beliefs indicate that the direction isn't reasonable). Notwithstanding, employees will sometimes be put into a compromised position. This dichotomy can lead to increased stress, strained relationships, or other challenges.

In this case, the reason provided to purchase the systems and maintenance didn't make sense. Although, there wasn't any evidence of any unethical actions, behaviors, or activities. Although there was angst and suspicion that something was extremely questionable. However, this belief wasn't sufficient to disobey an executive's direction.

This doesn't mean that anyone who considers an executive's direction to be questionable shouldn't seek other guidance, as guidance can be received from colleagues, managers, legal, human resources, the ethics compliance office, friends, etc.

Anyone who considers themselves to be in a compromised position should seek a second (and sometimes) a third opinion because dealing with questionable activities can be challenging.

The key message is that a failure to take reasonable action with knowledge about questionable activities isn't an excuse or a reason to be a party (willing or not) to unethical behavior.

Postlude

Prior to a mass layoff, the company had an extravagant off-site massive party that was referred to by some as the "last supper."

During this event, the company provided rooms of entertainment, along with several theme rooms with lots of different types of foods. A short time after this event, over 1/3 of the workforce nationwide was released on the same day.

Furthermore, the company in this case (along with its primary supplier) had a legal complaint filed against it by the Securities and Exchange Commission (SEC), which alleged fraud by both companies.

Unethical Activity Types:
- Character
- Illegal
- Intentional
- Morals
- Organizational
- Relational
- Societal
- Unintentional

Chapter 14:

Hiring Relatives or Friends
Without the Required Skills

Our team worked on strategic projects that (if not completed on-time) could create significant security challenges. The team was very small. Therefore, each team member had a significant workload. There was seldom any downtime on this team.

My role as the program manager was to ensure that the team understood the project's direction, issues were managed, resources were fully utilized, and much more.

One day the organization's director introduced a new team member. The team was happy to have an additional resource to relieve some of the workload. However, the team's excitement quickly turned to angst.

The team's angst was driven by the onboarding of a new team member who wasn't qualified for the job. This wasn't a casual observation, but one that was identified by the team's assessment about the new team member's technical, project management, and organizational knowledge.

As the program manager, I attempted to train this resource about the organization and project management prior to having this resource work on any technical issues. Unfortunately, the new team member didn't have the appropriate training or skills to be effective in the job without significant remedial training.

The team quickly realized and understood that this resource was hired based on a relationship with the director, which many team members suspected was due to nepotism.

Questions

1) Is it appropriate for a director to hire a close friend or relative to work directly for them? Why or why not?

2) How should someone deal with a team member that isn't qualified for a job?

3) What should be done to address someone who isn't doing their fair share of the work?

4) Would your answer to #3 above change if the individual in question was your manager? Why or why not?

5) Should the team discuss any concerns with the individual or the director? Why or why not?

6) If the issue is discussed with the individual or the director, what would be said?

7) What kinds of issues can be created if someone is unfairly given a position?

8) Would hiring an unqualified resource have a worse impact if the individual hired is related to the hiring manager? Why or why not?

Lessons Learned

Individuals will sometimes give an unfair advantage to a friend, family member, or significant other. These kinds of advantages aren't fair and can lead to organizational challenges (e.g., disgruntled employees, resignations).

Opportunities should be given based on an ability to deliver on expectations. However, other factors should be considered such as organizational fit, interpersonal skills, etc. Moreover, advantages shouldn't be given based on standards that can't be consistently applied.

Working with individuals who aren't qualified or don't contribute equally can be very frustrating. Furthermore, the usage of unfair standards can lead to other organizational issues, such as withdrawal, negative attitudes, interpersonal conflicts, etc.

Anyone who has concerns about arbitrary hiring practices has a right to address these concerns with a manager or human resources. Although, this kind of conversation might be handled best via a private conversation with human resources. This type of approach can be an effective strategy to prevent other interpersonal conflicts, especially with management.

Any concerns related to someone's skill or contributions shouldn't be discussed with the person subject to scrutiny, as this resource didn't make the hiring decision. Nor should the individual be subject to unnecessary attacks, which might impact their emotional well-being.

Life isn't always fair, and issues will generally not be resolved without action being taken to address the matter. Therefore, there isn't any point in complaining without taking action to resolve the issue. Therefore, individuals should put their efforts toward positive actions and improvements instead of wasting time complaining or speaking to individuals who can't change the situation.

Unethical Activity Types:
- Character
- Intentional
- Morals
- Organizational
- Relational

Chapter 15:

Using Past Working Dinners to Influence Future Actions

There are times that project teams will work late to accomplish a task or to complete a deliverable. During these times, teams might order dinner to be delivered to the office or leave the office to get something to eat. Regardless of the choice, at times, a single individual will pay the entire bill.

In this scenario, a vendor and the project team worked late nights to negotiate a contract, discuss technical strategy, or resolve implementation issues. Many times, the vendor would buy the team dinner since these were working meals.

The dinner contributions were a nice gesture but weren't expected or requested by the team. Notwithstanding, these late-night dinner meetings were usually very productive and allowed the team to resolve any program issues without unnecessary delay.

There was never a sense of an expectation of quid pro quo until late in the program at a time that the vendor needed to meet quarterly sales objectives. It was at this point that the vendor requested and demanded (through actions and behaviors) extraordinary efforts by me as the program manager to get a sales contract approval expedited in the last few days before the end-of-the-quarter.

This less than subtle request from the vendor was an uncomfortable experience. The vendor used considerable pressure on me to provide extra assistance to get the orders approved. Assistance was provided by me as it would be for any vendor. However, the support provided to the vendor wasn't beyond reasonable actions or expectations.

Questions

1) How should vendor requests for preferential treatment be handled?

2) Is it ever acceptable to give a vendor preferential treatment? Why or why not?

3) Should a vendor be allowed to pay for an employee's meal? Why or why not?

4) Might there be a time that it would be appropriate for a vendor to be allowed to pay for an employee's meal? If so, when? If not, why not?

5) Should the vendor's assertive behavior and request for extraordinary effort (to have its contract executed) be reported to management? Why or why not?

Lessons Learned

Requests will (at times) be made to benefit a party and may require extra effort to resolve. During these moments, there aren't normally any issues with aiding to complete a task or to achieve an objective. Although, any such requests should be reasonable and not be requested as payback for an earlier action, activity, or transaction.

There aren't any issues with a vendor requesting assistance, but a vendor shouldn't communicate (through activities) that repayment is required for any previous goodwill gesture.

In most cases, individuals should try to resolve issues directly unless doing so will damage a relationship, lead to further issues, or if the other party is in a much higher position. Any individual that is involved in an uncomfortable position shouldn't hesitate to get others' assistance.

Nobody should ever feel required to do something based on quid pro quo. Actions should happen and behaviors should occur because it is the right thing to do and not because of an expectation or a requirement to do something to meet other's personal objectives.

Unethical Activity Types:
- Character
- Morals
- Organizational
- Relational

Chapter 16:

Disparate Treatment

My "Introduction to Business" students are required to deliver individual presentations. On this night my lecture went a little long, and there was barely enough time to complete the scheduled presentations.

There were approximately ten minutes left in the class period, which wasn't enough time for another student to set-up, deliver, and answer questions about their presentation. However, in an attempt to not get behind in the next class, a student was asked to give their presentation in the remaining class time.

The issue created by allowing this student to present was that the student's presentation took almost fifteen minutes, which exceeded the ten-minute presentation time limit and the class period.

The student who presented last was given extra time to present, even though the presentation time limit was exceeded. The reason that the student was given extra time was due to the student being rushed to set-up and deliver the presentation under extra stress.

Immediately after the class, a student asked me, "Why was she given additional time to complete her presentation; is it because she's cute?" The comment received from the student was a surprise, as my intent was to give the student a little extra time due to being rushed to deliver a presentation with very little time remaining in the class period.

This accusation that I would treat students differently due to arbitrary factors bothered me greatly. Therefore, my options were evaluated about ways to handle this situation while also addressing the potential concerns of other students.

After some consideration, a decision was made rather quickly. My decision resulted in a teachable moment, along with a posted class announcement to the student's e-learning system prior to the next class. This announcement allowed me to address any other students' concerns without any further delay.

My announcement apologized for the perceived "disparate treatment," which allowed for a student to be treated differently due to arbitrary considerations. Also, my announcement provided the reason for the student being allowed to exceed the presentation time limit. Moreover, my students were permitted to discuss their concerns about preferential treatment during the next class period.

Questions

1) Should the student have been allowed to start their presentation with just a little more than ten minutes remaining in the class period? Why or why not?

2) Was it appropriate to allow a student to exceed the presentation time limit? Why or why not?

3) Is it ever appropriate to apply different rules for individuals within the same group?   If so, when might this be appropriate? If not, why not?

4) How would you respond to someone who accused you of disparate treatment or favoritism?

5) Is it ever appropriate to "break the rules?" Why or why not?

6) Was it appropriate to address the accusation of disparate treatment prior to the next class via an announcement? Why or why not?

7) Was there any benefit received by allowing other students (during the next class) to discuss any potential concerns about the extra time that was given to the student to present? Why or why not?

Lessons Learned

Unnecessarily putting a student on the spot to present under pressure to meet my needs to remain on schedule wasn't appropriate. Even if the student agreed (perhaps due to feeling pressured), it wasn't fair to the student who worked to deliver a quality presentation without any additional pressure.

At times, someone's activities should be evaluated to determine if there are any teachable moments.

In this case, the teachable moment for me was to always allow my students an opportunity to excel without any extra pressure. Also, there was an increased realization that someone's motives may be questioned if there is a perception of disparate or preferential treatment.

The lesson learned by my students is that a leader can make a mistake. Furthermore, no one (leader or not) should have concerns about acknowledging a mistake, taking action to correct it, sharing any lessons learned, and moving on from an issue as quickly as possible.

Some of the best times to demonstrate leadership are after a misstep (real or perceived). By allowing yourself to be vulnerable to acknowledge and admit an error in judgment, this kind of openness can lead to greater trust, opportunities to bond further, and strengthen connections to those under your purview.

Unethical Activity Types:

- Organizational
- Relational
- Societal
- Unintentional

Chapter 17:

Receiving Credit That Isn't Due

A colleague and I took a break to have lunch. During lunch, we discussed a company that we both were previously employed. Our discussion focused on a $25 phone bill credit ("phone credit") that was automatically received as an employee benefit while working at a telephone company.

During our conversation, I made a comment that I still received my phone credit on my personal phone bill. Then, my co-worker said, "I received my credit after I left also, but I called the company to get it canceled."

My reaction to this disclosure was embarrassment, as I realized that I had a responsibility to report to my former company that I still received the phone credit, which I was no longer eligible to receive.

After this conversation, I contacted my former company to have the phone credit canceled, also.

Questions

1) Would you report the receipt of a credit that was still received after it was no longer due to you? Why or why not?

2) How would this situation make you feel after your colleague disclosed that action was taken on their part to remove the credit (if you didn't do the same)? Why would you feel this way?

3) Could another individual's actions impact your behavior or decisions? Why or why not?

4) Might this situation impact the way you conducted your future affairs? Why or why not?

Lessons Learned

Lessons are sometimes learned at the most unexpected moments.

Someone's intent might not be to engage in unethical activities. However, the inability to process their activities (intended or not) isn't an excuse to not take action to do the "right thing."

It was understood that the credit was no longer due, but there wasn't an intent to defraud. The expectation was that this company's employee off-boarding would eventually stop the erroneous credit. However, there was a missed opportunity to proactively correct the issue.

Someone who takes a wait-and-see approach for an issue to resolve itself isn't the best solution. Individuals have a responsibility to correct any situation that isn't earned, deserved, or warranted, as everyone has a responsibility to act accordingly even if actions don't happen timely to resolve themselves.

Unethical Activity Types:
- Character
- Morals
- Relational
- Societal
- Unintentional

Chapter 18:

Accepting Loan Data Without Verifiable Applicant Information

While working on a contract assignment to implement a new web-based system, data that was representative of the types of data that would be processed by the system under development was required for testing. The director who was responsible for the functional area (and whose team would be a primary system user) negotiated with its suppliers to obtain actual data to be used for testing.

The issue with the data file was that there were numerous entries that didn't have all the required information to validate the individual's identity (e.g., social security number, physical address, job information). The missing information in the data file was questioned by me to the director. However, the director's answer was shocking and very surprising.

The director went on to tell me that the missing data was a normal occurrence. This disclosure was alarming, as this data was used to validate the identity, residence, and employment of the applicant. All of which were important to ensure that loans would be repaid.

This business practice was questioned, as there wasn't a way to validate, contact, or locate a loan applicant. However, the director wasn't concerned about this matter because the data originated from the financial institution's customer. Therefore, the director kept distance from any accountability and responsibility to ensure data integrity because the decision to accept the questionable data was made by a senior executive.

Questions

1) Are there any issues with using data that isn't accurate? Why or why not?

2) Should any action be taken to ensure quality data is received to protect the company's interest? Why or why not?

3) If you worked on this project, would you express your concerns about the data quality to the director? Why or why not?

4) Would your answer to #3 change if you were a contractor versus an employee? Why or why not?

5) What type of issues could be created for a company that uses erroneous data?

Lessons Learned

At times, processes will be followed even though there are known issues. However, this isn't an excuse to not take action to correct any flaws, especially if an unresolved issue has greater implications.

Anyone involved with a process has a responsibility to ensure quality and accurate data is used to the extent possible. It isn't acceptable to leave things the same because of a viewpoint that "This is the way it has always been done."

Everyone has a responsibility to take corrective action to resolve any questionable or unethical practices. Otherwise, unresolved issues can have unintended consequences for the team, organization, company, stakeholders, and society related to opportunity costs, increased prices for goods or services, lost revenue, and more.

Unethical Activity Types:
- Character
- Intentional
- Morals
- Organizational
- Relational

Chapter 19:

Changing Audit Results to Meet a Client's Needs

An audit is generally conducted to obtain information about or validate systems, processes, procedures, compliance, or other factors. Some audits are performed in an open format and others are conducted with lots of controls to obtain unbiased or influenced results.

On this task, the goals and objectives were to evaluate the organization's process maturity, capabilities, and readiness to implement a major system replacement. This audit specifically required an independent controlled process to obtain an evaluation of the organization without any influence from any of the organization's members.

After the interviews, system/process reviews, and data collection were completed, the audit results were compiled. The process to complete the audit report was very intensive and cumbersome, as it took several weeks to complete the initial results. The next step (once the initial report was completed) was to meet with the client's representatives to review the initial audit results.

The review of the initial audit results went well. There weren't any significant issues identified by the client's representatives or the senior team in which the results were reviewed. Generally, the initial results are delivered during this meeting and the report is considered 85 - 95% complete. At this point in the process, there are normally not any major changes made to the report after this meeting.

The next meeting with the client occurred after the delivery of the final report. The purpose of this meeting was to review the audit results with the client's executive team and strategic organizational members.

As the final report and presentation were prepared, the client's representatives requested that the audit results be materially changed to convey information that wasn't identified during the audit. Also, there was a request from the same representatives to communicate a shortage of resources (e.g., financial, human) that wasn't identified as part of the audit analysis.

The most likely reason that the client wanted the audit results changed was that this report was to be delivered during a major downturn in the economy, which made obtaining project funding more difficult. A contributing factor to this belief is that the client didn't request any changes to the audit report nor identify any concerns with the draft report during the initial review. Furthermore, the requested changes were made during the client's budget review for the upcoming year.

My concerns about and resistance to making material changes to the audit results (that didn't reflect the findings) were communicated to my employer's executive team. Initially the executive team agreed with my position. However, the executive's position changed after the client threatened future business if the results weren't updated as requested to meet its needs.

My executive team (after several follow-up discussions) directed me to change the audit results to meet the client's needs. After the executive team's direction was received, I communicated (as the audit lead) to the executive my displeasure and frustration about the company's willingness to compromise its position and integrity for revenue.

My feelings about this situation were exacerbated because prior to the client's (a major revenue contributor) threats related to the company's ability to obtain future business, the executive team agreed with each other and me that the audit results shouldn't be changed.

At this point, I took time to determine if I would follow my beliefs to not manipulate the independent audit results to meet the client's needs or to continue my employment with this company ... there weren't any other options, as the executive team had already made its decision.

If I remained at this company and changed the audit results, I wouldn't be "true" to myself and would do something against my ethical beliefs[7].

If I didn't make the changes and left the company, I would remain "true" to myself, my beliefs, and would also be unemployed. If I did make the changes, then I wouldn't be "true" to myself or my beliefs and would remain employed.

My decision wasn't a difficult decision. However, I wanted to delay any action until after some time had passed to carefully consider my decision.

It is important to note that another option presented to the executive team was to include a statement in the audit report that documented that the client was a participant in the determination of material information that would be included in the client's deliverables. My offer was rejected, as the executives didn't want to include any disclaimer in the audit report. Therefore, my decision on my next steps (for all

---

[7] Reference the article " Are You Really Who You Think You Are?" in Appendix D.

practical purposes) was made by the executive's decision.

That evening I decided to resign from the company instead of doing something that I considered to be questionable or unethical, would materially change the audit results, and would no longer make the audit results independent. After my decision, I wrote my resignation letter and placed it on a counter near my front-door. The final step to confirm my decision was to sleep on my decision. Then, if I felt the same way the next morning, I would resign.

The next morning, I took my resignation letter to work and resigned. My choice and subsequent decision to resign was difficult as I enjoyed the job. However, I couldn't keep a job at the cost of doing something that didn't align with my moral, ethical, or spiritual beliefs.

Questions

1) Would you change information to meet a client's business needs if a request didn't align with the audit and analysis conducted?

2) Would your answer to the previous question change if an executive at the company you worked for directed the change? Why or why not?

3) Is it ever appropriate to do something to meet a client's needs that you don't agree? If so, when might this be appropriate? If not, why not?

4) Is it ever appropriate to not follow executive direction? If so, when might this be appropriate? If not, why not?

5) Are there any other options that might be available to resolve this situation? If so, what? If not, why not?

Lessons Learned

Audits are conducted to obtain an analysis about an organization's, process, systems, financials, compliance, and more. If an audit is independent, individuals who are part of the audit process shouldn't be included in the process to create the audit results. Although, participation in the audit process is normally permissible. Furthermore, any involvement beyond that necessary to compile data to complete an audit or to clarify audit findings should be disclosed.

Organizational dynamics can be a significant factor with compliance. Executives are the organization's leaders and as such set the standard for behavioral compliance. If an organization's leaders don't demonstrate a commitment to ethical activities, then this can create a barrier for organizational ethical behavior and compliance.

Regardless of executive direction, everyone must make a personal choice whether to be ethical or not. Environmental conditions may influence someone's decision-making process. However, a decision whether to be ethical is still an individual choice.

Once a decision is made, the person must be responsible and accountable for their actions. However, there are times that individuals may experience stress or duress to act in a certain way, but ultimately there's always a choice that drives their action.

The choices and decisions someone makes while being pressured to do something counter to their beliefs reflects who the individual chooses (actively or passively) to be.

Unethical Activity Types:
- Character
- Illegal
- Intentional
- Morals
- Relational
- Societal

Chapter 20:
Questionable Business Practices

There was a lot of excitement after an employment offer was received to work as a government contractor. This job had a lot of potential to work on some interesting and challenging projects, along with the receipt of a very generous salary. The issue was that there was very little work assigned. At first, my time was spent getting system access and assembling budget information.

The first issue identified while working on a project budget was that the director who controlled a significant portion of the operational expenses wouldn't return my messages (phone or email). After a couple of days of not getting a response, my onsite director was notified about the issue. After my onsite director got involved, a meeting was scheduled with the elusive director.

The excitement about getting the meeting scheduled quickly turned to angst as the director told me to use arbitrary budget information that was provided without any validation. Submitting budget numbers without any validation was against everything I was taught about creating a budget, along with my ethical concerns about this action.

After the meeting, my concerns about the receipt of questionable operational costs were discussed with my onsite director who noted my concerns. However, the budget was submitted without any corrections. My onsite director's emphasis appeared to be focused on receipt of recognition for the completion of the budget information versus being concerned about the faulty data.

The issues with this director's organization were that there wasn't enough work to do or assigned. Also, this director seemed to be trying to build a sizable organization for status reasons (as other individuals didn't have enough work to do either).

Most of my time was spent sitting at my desk without any work to do. This wasn't my preferred situation as I enjoy being fully engaged with my work. This is the reason that I would often request work assignments, but there wasn't any work assigned to me.

Feeling desperate to do something, I tried to schedule meetings with some of the directors that worked with our team. However, responses to my meeting requests were seldom received. Then, I pleaded with my onsite director to schedule meetings with the directors which we worked to identify work for me to do. The director reluctantly scheduled a couple of meetings. Unfortunately, nothing came from these meetings. During a separate conversation with a colleague on my team after requesting work to do, this colleague said, "You'll get used to it."

In addition to not having any work assigned for myself or other contractors, my onsite director continued to expand the team. My observation was that my director's objective was to increase the size of the team to demonstrate the director's importance.

My concerns about the budget data collection process and not having any work to do were reported to my contracting company. However, there wasn't any willingness to intervene, as my job was a strategic position in the organization that could lead to additional billable positions on this team.

This type of business relationship can challenge ethical

principles because if this contracting company addressed the resource underutilization issue, this could impact the contracting company's ability to secure additional work and impact its revenue. This type of conflict can lead to decisions that are counter to the client's organizational goals to maximize the return-on-investment.

As my onsite director's team size grew, my frustrations about not being assigned any work increased also until I decided to resign. The reason that I chose to resign was that I: a) didn't want to be at work without any work to complete, b) was paid a significant salary to not complete any work, and c) wasted taxpayer money (including mine).

Questions

1) What would you do if it was your responsibility to collect budget data and the information received for the budget was known to be inaccurate?

2) Whose responsibility is it to ensure that the budget information submitted is accurate? Why do the individuals identified have this role?

3) What would you do if you weren't assigned any work to complete and spent most of the day not performing any work? Why is this approach acceptable?

4) Should anything be done if it is observed that your manager increased their team's size for appearance purposes only? Why or why not?

5) Is submitting budget data that isn't validated ethical? Why or why not?

6) Is it unethical to be paid to not complete any work? Why or why not?

7) Is it fraudulent to be paid to not complete any work? Why or why not?

8) Would your answers to #6 and #7 change if you worked as a government contractor versus an employee?

Lessons Learned

Everyone has a responsibility to protect company resources and to ensure that resources are used in the best manner possible to maximize the return-on-investment.

Furthermore, it isn't an acceptable practice to knowingly submit budget data that isn't validated (to the extent possible) to be accurate. Otherwise, data that is submitted without validation can impact reporting accuracy, cost accounting, expense management, the potential for cost overruns, and more.

As for not having any work assigned, individuals should attempt to remain as productive as possible. Notwithstanding, it is understood that there will be times that work will have moments that aren't as productive, but these periods of downtime shouldn't occur that often. During these moments, individuals should identify (on their own, with help from management, or from other sources) ways to maximize their productivity.

Everyone has a responsibility to ensure that resources (e.g., workers, funding) are used as effectively as possible. If not, action should be taken to resolve the issue as soon as practical to prevent any unnecessary waste.

Unethical Activity Types:

- Character
- Cultural
- Illegal
- Intentional
- Morals
- Organizational
- Relational
- Societal
- Unintentional

Chapter 21

Every Student
Receives a Perfect Grade

After being assigned to teach a new course, another professor was shadowed to review the way their course was taught. This approach was an effective strategy to review the course material, be mentored by a senior professor, and review this professor's methodology to teach the course.

While reviewing this professor's online gradebook, there was an interesting discovery. All of this instructor's students (approximately 35) received perfect scores for every assignment, which was highly questionable. Some of the student's submissions barely met the assignment's submission requirements.

After further review, it was also discovered that the grades entered for each assignment were entered within seconds of each other. The quick entry of the grades wasn't necessarily an issue, as a professor might grade assignments outside of the system and post everyone's grades at the same time. Nevertheless, it was still questionable that every student earned a perfect score.

After thinking about the number of perfect scores for a while, options were considered about the best method to address this situation. The first option was to discuss this issue with another professor. The second option was to discuss this issue with the head of the organization. The third option was to report this issue anonymously. The fourth option was to discuss the issue with the professor in question. My initial decision was to discuss the issue with another professor.

The grading issue was discussed with another professor without any disclosure about who assigned perfect grades to each student. The advice received from this professor reflected my thoughts about the issue, which was that each student should be graded based on the merits of their work. Furthermore, it was highly unlikely that every student would receive a perfect grade. This is the reason that there was agreement that the issue must be reported to administration for review.

The reasons that it was important to report my grading concerns are that: (a) it wasn't fair that students received grades that weren't based on the merits of their work, (b) each professor had a responsibility to thoughtfully review and grade assignments, (c) the school's accreditation could be impacted by reports of grading concerns or inflation, (d) employers and other schools use the grades as an evaluation of a student's mastery of the material, (e) it's unethical.

Based on these reasons, a meeting was scheduled with the head of the organization to discuss my grading concerns. During the meeting, the grading issues observed were discussed. However, due to the progression of the conversation, it wasn't hopeful that any real action would be taken to resolve my grading concerns. My belief was validated about a year later once the professor's course was reviewed by me as part of a course evaluation. At that time, the professor in question was still recording perfect grades to students on all homework assignments.

Questions

1) Is it an issue for a professor to give every student a perfect grade? Why or why not?

2) Should any action be taken if it is discovered that a professor gave every student a perfect grade? If so, what? If not, why not?

3) How would you handle the discovery of grade assignment or inflation issues?

4) Would a potential grade assignment issue be handled differently if you were friends with the professor? Why or why not?

5) Should the grading concerns be reported? Why or why not?

6) If a decision was made to report the grading issue, how would the issue be reported (directly, indirectly, or anonymously)? Why was the reporting method chosen?

7) If a decision was made to not report the grading issue, what would prevent you from reporting the issue?

Lessons Learned

Individuals will sometimes be faced with a choice whether to act on knowledge about an unethical issue or not. During these times, individuals are faced with a difficult choice to decide whether to get involved. Anyone who chooses to address unethical activities can feel considerable pressure about their willingness to get involved. Conversely, individuals who have knowledge about ethical issues and don't report it become complicit to the act.

Addressing ethical issues doesn't mean that someone must personally act. However, individuals have a responsibility to ensure that unethical activities are reported so that it can be resolved accordingly, even if it is reported anonymously.

Unethical activities don't only affect the individual who commits the offense, as their activities can also have an impact on their colleagues, the team, the organization, and sometimes external impacts, as well. This is a reason that unethical behavior should be reported in a timely manner, which will also reduce the damage that can be caused if any unethical activities go unchallenged, unreported, or unresolved.

Unethical Activity Types:
- Character
- Intentional
- Morals
- Organizational
- Relational
- Societal

Chapter 22:
Stop the Timer

Drive-through windows were created for customer convenience and productivity enhancement. Therefore, employees who work drive-through windows will attempt to meet productivity measurements based on their ability to process as many customers as quickly as possible.

The normal process is to order food at a speaker and then drive to a window to pay and pick-up the processed food order. However, at times, the process can be different than its most likely designed.

For example, some employees have modified the drive-through process as follows:

a) place an order and be directed by the employee to wait at the speaker until instructed to drive to the next window;

b) place an order, drive to the next window to pay, and be directed to drive past the window to wait for the order to be brought to the car.

After experiencing this practice of being directed to drive past the pick-up window a few times without any waiting customers in line, an employee was asked about the reason for having customers drive past the pick-up window to wait for food to be brought to their car. The response received was that there was a timer at the window and the drive-through employees were measured on the amount of time it took to serve customers. The timer tracked the amount of time from an entered order until the customer received their order at the pick-up window.

This disclosure identified and validated my belief that some employees manipulated the defined process to decrease a productivity measurement, specifically the amount of time it took to process a customer order.

Questions

1) Are there any issues with a drive-through employee modifying the process and/or procedures to meet their needs?

2) Is it appropriate for an employee to change a defined process or procedure? If so, why? If not, why not?

3) Is it appropriate for an employee to change a defined process or procedure with a goal to manipulate the performance measurement? If so, why? If not, why not?

4) What might it suggest about an employee's or an organization's mindset if data is intentionally manipulated to meet performance goals?

Lessons Learned

Individuals involved with a process will sometimes manipulate the process or procedures to meet their needs or objectives. Actions similar to those identified in this case might not be sanctioned by management or the organization. However, individuals may use knowledge of the controls used to manage a process or procedure to manipulate the results if there is an opportunity.

Organizations must ensure that proper controls are implemented to prevent the potential for individuals to work outside of the process or procedural norms. If controls aren't properly implemented, some individuals will use this knowledge to manipulate the process or procedures to meet their needs and not the needs of the organization.

The implementation of periodic, unannounced audits will provide opportunities to validate process or procedural compliance. These types of audits can minimize opportunities to and serve as a deterrent for unethical activities.

Unethical Activity Types:
- Character
- Intentional
- Morals
- Organizational
- Relational

Chapter 23:

Workplace Abuse

As the contracted program manager for a large software development program, there was a need to hire a significant number of contractors to complete system testing. Therefore, during the early phase of the program, the onsite manager provided me with the authority to obtain the necessary resources. My authority included interaction with contracting companies to review resumes, schedule interviews, and conduct interviews.

During the initial review of candidates, some of the contracting companies complained to this organization's contracting office that a contractor was involved with the hiring decision for other contractors. The major concern raised by the contracting company's was that the open positions would be unfairly directed to the contracting company that I worked, which this idea wasn't even considered by me.

After the contracting companies' complaint, my onsite manager told me that the only way that a contract program manager (me) could make a hiring decision for another consultant was if an employee of this organization was part of the consultant selection process. The reason that this change was required was to ensure that my actions were monitored to not give an unfair advantage to the contracting company that I worked.

The new direction received by my onsite manager was followed. However, this process change didn't have any added value as the contractor's selection decision was still made by me as the program manager. The only benefit that came from this change was that an organizational employee was added to the interview process to monitor my interviews, but not my actions or decisions. This change was made to manage perceptions, but the change didn't have any impact on the original process used to select consultants.

A short time later, my onsite manager directed me to review resumes from a contracting company that a friend of this manager's spouse worked. This company wasn't an authorized contracting company. However, there was a way to circumvent the normal and approved contractor lists to add additional companies to the authorized contracting company list through exception processing.

The addition of this contracting company allowed my onsite manager to direct work to the manager's spouse's friend's company, which was a questionable act.

This situation was laughable since the selection process used was changed to minimize any questionable or unethical activity by me. Then, after the selection process was modified, my onsite manager's actual behavior was questionable or unethical because my onsite manager's actions were the same as those that the contracting companies were concerned that I would do.

Questions

1) Was it appropriate to add an extra level of control to prevent a contractor from directing work to their contracting company? If so, why? If not, why not?

2) Were there other options that could be implemented instead of adding an extra level of control? If so, what? If not, why not?

3) What are your thoughts about an onsite manager directing work to a spouse's friend's company?

4) Would your answer to #3 be different if action was recently taken to prevent you from directing work to the company that you worked? Why or why not?

5) Should the onsite manager's questionable or unethical activity be reported? Why or why not?

Lessons Learned

Companies should take proactive action to minimize any opportunities for unethical activities. Otherwise, any opportunities for unethical activities can provide temptations for individuals to act and/or behave inappropriately. Furthermore, companies should periodically review processes and procedures to determine if any changes might be needed or required to reflect any changes to business operations.

Process changes (e.g., process, procedural, system) should be proactively reviewed, implemented, and tested to ensure that no other gaps exist instead of limiting solutions to the current known issue(s). Moreover, any process changes should be fully tested to ensure that no other gaps exist after making a change. Otherwise, additional changes might need to be made, or individuals will identify other gaps within a process to exploit.

Processes and procedures should be sufficiently audited to minimize opportunities to engage in questionable or unethical activities.

It's important to remember that any implemented controls, ethical activities, and choices ultimately begin and end with an individual and whether the person has a desire to be ethical.

Unethical Activity Types:

- Character
- Cultural
- Intentional
- Morals
- Organizational
- Relational

Chapter 24:

An Unnecessary

Verbal Attack

A project team meeting was held to discuss development activities for an upcoming system implementation. At the meeting, there were a significant number of team members in the meeting room, as well as via a conference call.

During this meeting, a well-respected senior team member participated in the project discussions until the team member was abruptly interrupted. The interruption was very callous, as a company executive told the senior team member to basically "shut-up and not say another word." This behavior was shocking. However, this type of aggressive behavior was customary for this executive.

At other times, this senior executive would attack anyone who didn't agree with or support the executive's views. However, this organization sanctioned the behavior by allowing it to occur. The most likely reason that this executive was permitted to behave this way was due to the executive's significant operational knowledge or that the management team was intimidated by this executive.

This executive's unacceptable activities were reported to the senior management team who appeared to not take any corrective action because the behavior continued.

Questions

1) What would you do if someone told you to "shut-up and not say another word?" Would your reaction be different if the speaker was an executive?

2) Would your reaction to the comments be different if you were a temporary employee versus a direct-hire employee? Why or why not?

3) If the resource that was told to "shut-up" was embarrassed, humiliated, or demeaned by the behavior, but didn't report the incident to their management... would you report the incident on their behalf? Why or why not?

4) Is it ever acceptable for a manager to tell a direct report to "shut-up?" If so, when? If not, why not?

5) If someone witnesses derogatory behavior and doesn't report it, is the witness complicit? Why or why not?

Lessons Learned

It is never acceptable for anyone to treat someone in a derogatory manner. There are many different and effective ways to get someone to stop unwanted behavior other than to embarrass, humiliate, demean, threaten, or antagonize.

Anyone who is treated in a manner that is unacceptable should address or report the activity, as nobody should have to tolerate any unwelcome, unwanted, or aggressive behavior. Companies should have documented policies and procedures for any resource (employee, contract, and temporary personnel) to report any unacceptable activities (even anonymously, as some individuals may be fearful of retaliation if the attacks are reported).

Furthermore, companies should take swift action to resolve any aggressive or unwanted activities to resolve the issue in a timely manner. Otherwise, the ongoing behavior may create a hostile work environment that impacts the individual, organization, and company. In severe cases, a company's response may include the removal of the attacker from the environment until the incident can be properly documented, investigated, and resolved.

Nobody should have to deal with, tolerate, or address any abusive environments alone. For this reason, it is imperative that companies take immediate action to protect its resources.

Unethical Activity Types:

- Character
- Cultural
- Intentional
- Morals
- Organizational
- Relational
- Societal

Chapter 25:

Academic Dishonesty

College students can have a lot of assignments to complete during the semester. The benefits of receiving different types of assignments are for students to apply the course concepts; also, assignments can be beneficial to determine if there is consistency with a student's work.

There's normally not a purposeful intention to search for assignments that are plagiarized during my classes. However, at times, it is noticeable that there is a change in the student's writing style. During these times, the questionable assignments are normally processed through a plagiarism checking system to determine if the material submitted is original work. The system used to scrutinize assignments isn't perfect, but it provides an opportunity to check assignments that appear to be inconsistent with a student's previous work.

In this example, a student completed an 8-week course within a couple weeks after the course started, except for the group project and the final exam. The student's assignments that were submitted early weren't graded until all other assignments were graded during the week the assignments were due.

At the end of the course, the student's final exam was scrutinized because the writing appeared to be inconsistent with previously submitted work. Also, the student completed a semester's worth of work in a very short period.

The last assignment prior to the final exam was to write about the lessons learned in the course, which the student completed in the first couple of weeks. The early submission of the lessons learned is the reason that the student was asked to redo this assignment at the end versus the beginning of the course. This request didn't go over well with the student who became aggressive, derogatory, and personally attacked me on email.

A short time later prior to grading final exams, it was noticed that the writing on the student's section of the group project was different than previous submissions. Therefore, the student's assignments were reviewed via a plagiarism checking system to determine if the work was plagiarized.

After the plagiarism check was completed, a report was generated which detailed that over 75% of the student's work was plagiarized. This is the reason that a few of the student's assignments were also checked for plagiarism, which the results of the analysis were approximately the same as the initial assignment that was checked.

Normally, after a discovery that a student plagiarized work, a discussion about plagiarism would be had with the student. Then, the student would be directed to write an essay about the reason that plagiarizing another's work is unacceptable. However, this student's nasty and belligerent behavior started to get worse. As this student's antics increased, this student began to make insults about my character on email, along with instructing me not to contact the student again.

During the time of this student's attacks against me (and unrelated to the student's behaviors), this student was assigned an "F" on each of the assignments that were plagiarized. After being notified about the posting of these grades, this student then used the college's appeal process to question the failing grades.

After exhausting the appeal process, the student received an "F" in my course. The unfortunate part is that the student would have been given an opportunity for redemption had the student remained calm and admitted that their work was plagiarized. Instead, the student took action that resulted in no other option but to assign an "F" as the course grade since the college's appeal process was used.

Questions

1) What would you do if a student's assignments were plagiarized?

2) If a student was given a chance for redemption, why would this be done? If a student wasn't given a chance for redemption, why wouldn't this be done?

3) What would you do if a student became aggressive and attacked your character after discovering that their assignments were plagiarized?

4) Would a student's personal attacks affect the way the student was treated? Why or why not?

5) Was there an opportunity to teach this student a lesson based on their unacceptable behavior? If so, what could be taught? If not, why not?

6) Do you agree with the result? Why or why not?

Lessons Learned

Submitting another's work as your own isn't an acceptable practice.

This student had an opportunity to admit that their assignments were plagiarized. However, while faced with documented evidence this student chose to become aggressive, derogatory, and use personal insults toward the individual who discovered the plagiarism. None of the behaviors by this student were acceptable, nor did it reflect any personal accountability or responsibility.

The best action the student could have taken after the violation of the student code was discovered was to admit that assignments were plagiarized. Then, the student could deal with the consequences, ask for forgiveness, and not plagiarize others' work again.

By accepting accountability and responsibility, this type of admission might lead to favorable treatment or an opportunity for redemption. Moreover, further denials and bad behaviors may prevent someone with the power and authority to assist from acting positively in someone's favor.

The best option is for individuals to not unnecessarily put themselves in compromised positions that would require an apology, redemption, and another's assistance, which may also prevent negative documentation from being added to someone's record.

Unethical Activity Types

- Character
- Cultural
- Intentional
- Morals
- Organizational
- Relational
- Societal

Chapter 26:

Company Responsibility

Companies have a responsibility to establish policies and procedures, including ethical standards. Also, during an onboarding and indoctrination to a company, resources (e.g., employees, contractors) should be trained on acceptable and expected behavioral standards.

All management levels, especially executive management, must set an example and standard for all resources to follow.

Organizations should do the following to minimize unethical activities:

- Demonstrate ethical activities in all transactions, interactions, and communication

- Create ethics policies and standards related to appropriate ethical activities

- Enforce any policy or standards timely, fairly, and without retaliation

- Discuss behavioral expectations within each manager's team at least twice a year

- Review policies and standards annually to determine if updates are required

Companies should provide periodic ethics training, which will reinforce acceptable ethical activities. Furthermore, situational training can assist teams to improve their understanding of ethical dilemmas, conflict of interests, ethical issue management, including processes and procedures to report ethical issues.

Companies that don't maintain environments (for resources to be ethical and maintain high ethical standards) should expect activities that lead to inappropriate disclosures, questionable business arrangements, theft, embezzlement, and retaliation... including workplace bullying.

Chapter 27:

Individual Responsibility

Acting and behaving responsibly is something everyone should do regardless of pressure(s) to do otherwise. Furthermore, engaging in unethical activities due to direction(s) received isn't an acceptable (and shouldn't be a permissive) excuse for noncompliance with policy, process, procedural guidance, or expectations. Everyone should be held responsible and accountable for their choices.

Unethical activities should always be dealt with or reported as quickly as possible to minimize the possibility and opportunity for recurrence.

Actions that should be taken to address unethical activities:

- Become familiar with the types of unethical violations (described in Chapter 7)

- Review policies or standards to understand the way unethical activities are addressed

- Demonstrate ethical activities to serve as an ethical role model

- Keep a record of any unethical activities or incidents, including dates, times, and a factual description

- Report any unethical activities to someone with the authority (e.g., supervisor, manager, human resources) to create a formal record about any incident(s), which can also be reported anonymously

Employees shouldn't be afraid to document, question, or report questionable or unethical activities, even if it's done anonymously (as all employees have a responsibility to ensure that a company is protected against unnecessary fraud, theft, or other inappropriate conduct).

Unethical activities that aren't reported can lead to incidents that continue, get worse, or impact others. Moreover, unethical conduct can't be properly addressed unless it's identified, documented, and addressed (timely).

Chapter 28:

Ethical Violations

Impact on Others

Questionable or unethical activities can impact anyone (internal or external to the organization) if it isn't properly addressed. Many times, the issues associated with these types of activities aren't known or fully understood primarily due to these issues being ignored, not reported, underreported, or purposely hidden.

Potential issues created by questionable or unethical activities:

- Conflict – disagreements as to whether something is ethical

- Duress – pressure to do something someone knows isn't the correct thing to do

- Employee Dissatisfaction – impact on someone's positive beliefs about an organization, individuals within it, and/or processes and procedures used to address ethical concerns

- Gossip – rumors are spread about perceived or actual activities

- Impact on Morale – organizations that or individuals who engage in questionable and/or unethical activities can impact employee beliefs and heighten any concerns about the working environment

- Job Change – an employee might change their position or career instead of being involved with an organization and/or individual(s) who aren't ethical

- <u>Individual Impact</u> – a negative impact on someone's attitude about the work environment and sometimes life

- <u>Loss of Productivity/Efficiency</u> – time is used to discuss perceived or actual issues instead of working

- <u>Name Calling</u> – someone is negatively labeled for the report of unethical activities

- <u>Relationship Changes</u> – the nature of a relationship changes due to someone's activities

- <u>Resignation</u> – an employee might resign instead or being involved with someone or an organization that's unethical

- <u>Self-Doubt</u> – someone wonders whether their or others' activities are ethical

- <u>Stress</u> – someone experiences physical, mental, and/or emotional impacts during and while deciding whether the unethical activity should be reported

- <u>Transference</u> - impact to quality of life away from work (e.g., ability to relax, becoming distant with loved ones)

- <u>Weight Loss/Gain</u> – change (sometimes suddenly) in someone's physical appearance

This is a partial list of possible impacts that questionable, or activities can have on those affected and/or effected by unethical actors.

It's important that anyone who is aware of questionable or unethical activities report it. This will ensure that toxic or destructive behaviors are addressed as soon as practicable. Furthermore, companies should also have a zero-tolerance policy for any unethical activities, along with providing specific guidance about ways to address and prevent it. This includes ensuring that there are timely disclosures about any potential conflict(s) of interest(s).

Chapter 29:

Ethical Violations Statistics

Based on the Ethics Resource Center's (ERC) National Business Ethics Survey (NBES)[8], approximately 41% of respondents observed some type of misconduct and 63% of those who observed misconduct reported it. However, according to this survey, more than 1 in 5 workers who reported misconduct experienced some type of retaliation after reporting it.

These statistics are alarming as over 20% of those who report misconduct experience retaliation.

Another interesting observation based on the NBES is that misconduct normally doesn't happen just once. Based on the findings, 67% of misconduct is related to multiple incidents or ongoing patterns of behavior, which represents 41% and 26%, respectively. Furthermore, the NBES documents that 53% of misconduct is related to multiple individuals (41%) or a company-wide issue (12%).

The findings highlight that a large portion of the misconduct (over 50%) resulted from issues related to gift-giving, bribes, and political contributions.

The top incidents of retaliation based on the 2013 NBES:

- Treated differently or ignored by supervisors or other employees

- Excluded from decisions and work activities

[8] Ethics Resource Center (ERC). "National Business Ethics Survey of the U.S. Workforce" (2014). Used with ERC's permission, 2345 Crystal Drive, Suite 201, Arlington, Virginia 22202. Online (ethics.org), Retrieved: 3/14/14.

- Verbally abused by a manager or co-worker

- Almost fired, hours reduced, or experienced a base-pay reduction

Therefore, there's still work that must be done to minimize, prevent, and train individuals about the impacts of questionable or unethical activities.

Information about the ERC methodology used for the National Business Ethics Survey (NBES):

- Survey conducted September 30 – November 15, 2013

- Responses collected from a random sample of 6,579 employees over the age of 18 and employed at least 20 hours a week

- Responses received from 159 government or non-profit sector employees were removed to isolate for-profit employees, which left responses from 6,420 for-profit employees that were used for the survey results

- Sampling error of the findings in the NBES is +/-1.2% with a 95% confidence level

Chapter 30:
Underreporting of
Ethical Violations

The number of unethical activities is most likely much higher than the reported incidents. The most probable reason for lower reported incidents is that impacted parties don't want to get involved or fear retaliation.

Questionable or unethical activities might not be reported due to:

- Fear – the expectation that something bad will happen if an issue is reported

- Job Loss - loss of employment due to reporting of an issue

- Perception – belief that nothing will change if an issue is reported or that others will think negatively about someone who reports issues

- Reporting Process - the method to report an issue isn't understood

- Retaliation - backlash experienced by someone who reports an issue, including workplace bullying[9]

- Lack of Clarity About Rights – incorrect belief(s) that activities are based on a management style. Therefore, an employee must deal with these behaviors instead of being involved with resolving any issues

---

[9] Young, S. L. Bullies... They're In Your Office, Too... Could you be one? Arlington, Virginia: Beyond SPRH, LLC, 2013 – 2014, 2023 - 2024. Print.

It's important that companies remove barriers to addressing and/or reporting questionable or unethical activities to ensure ethical, honest, trustworthy, and safe work environments.

Chapter 31:
Costs of Not Reporting Unethical Activities

Questionable or unethical activities aren't always reported due to fears of retaliation, getting involved, perception, peer pressure, or other reasons. At times, some individuals won't get involved because there's a belief that if the incident doesn't have a direct impact on them than it's none of their business. Unfortunately, this belief is fundamentally incorrect, as ethical compliance is everyone's business and responsibility.

Anyone who has knowledge about an issue and doesn't report it is also culpable for the related questionable or unethical activities. Moreover, it must be clearly understood that questionable or unethical activities (whether reported or not) have a cost (direct and indirect) to individuals, organizations, and stakeholder value.

Impacts of not reporting any questionable or unethical issues:

- Actual – the amount associated with the damage caused by unethical activities

- Company – adverse impacts to a company's reputation, trustworthiness, business practices, and its operations

- Individual – stalled careers, negative interactions, and lost income

- Organizational – reduced standing to an organization's reputation, policies/procedures, and decision-making

- Productivity/Morale – employees who are concerned about ethical issues might use work time to discuss their concerns, worry about any issues, or other impacts instead of being engaged in their work

- <u>Reputational</u> – damage to the internal and external reputation of individuals, organizations, and companies involved with unethical issues

- <u>Team</u> – impact of unethical issues on a group's internal dynamics

- <u>Trust</u> – concerns about the honesty and integrity of a work effort

- <u>Unintended</u> – cost to take corrective action to resolve ethical issues, along with the operational time required to investigate and update controls (e.g., processes, procedures, audits, reporting)

Expenses related to addressing unethical issues extend well-beyond the cost of any negative actions or behaviors. Unethical activities often begin with the presence of an opportunity, which can be managed, minimized, or prevented with the implementation of stringent controls. Therefore, policies, processes, and procedures must be proactively implemented, monitored, tested, and reported. This ongoing practice will aid in the removal of many opportunistic moments for anyone to act and/or behave unethically.

Chapter 32:
Helping the
Ethically Challenged

Individuals might or might not realize that their activities are questionable or unethical. However, it's still everyone's responsibility to ensure that unethical activities are addressed as quickly as possible. If not, then issues remain unresolved and could lead to additional unethical activities.

Unethical individuals can be helped by:

- Counseling – the use of professional resources to attempt to identify and modify the sources of unethical activities

- Mentoring – partner individuals with well-respected resources who emulate the desired ethical activities

- Training – teach individuals about ways to accomplish their work without being unethical

- Terminating – individuals who can't or are unwilling to change their unethical activities must be removed from an organization

Questionable or unethical activities must be addressed timely. Otherwise, the negative impact(s) of these activities can lead to additional organizational challenges, such as a lack of trust, disparate treatment, others emulating the unwanted activity, judgments questioned, or different challenges.

Chapter 33:

Parting Thoughts

Making a choice to be ethical involves considerations about activities that are "good or bad" or "right or wrong." Many times, individuals know if their activities are ethical. The part that's grey is in the individual interpretation. However, at times, there can be moments in which a situation must be explored further to determine if it is or isn't ethical.

For example, at a recreational event I had a conversation with someone who asked me, "Who is your ethical role model?" I immediately replied, "Me, as I don't need an ethical role model because I know whether my behavior is "right or wrong," "good or bad," or if my activities are questionable."

Everyday individuals encounter pressures to get good grades, achieve sales quotas, make productivity targets, or pursue other measurements. These daily pressures can sometimes be so overwhelming that it causes individuals who would normally act/behave properly to make a bad choice/decision during a stressful or tempting moment.

Nevertheless, situational pressures aren't an excuse to act and/or behave unethically. Dealing with, addressing, and resolving stressful situations are a part of life. Therefore, individuals must learn coping skills to handle periodic challenges without having to use unethical methods to achieve their goals or objectives.

Throughout my life, I was always taught to "do the right thing" because someone's actions and behaviors reflect their character. Moreover, I was taught that every individual is responsible and accountable for their activities, regardless of any pressures or temptations to do otherwise. This guidance is true. Although, nobody told me that doing the "right thing" could have a negative, personal, and (sometimes) substantial cost.

During my college business classes as a student, there were discussions about ethical dilemmas that influenced my (and most likely my classmates') future ethical behavior. The general themes of these discussions were to "do the right thing" and "report unethical activities."

Despite these lessons, I wasn't prepared during my professional career for the reactions, backlash, and issues that would be encountered due to taking a stand against unethical activities. My disappointed realization was that it's much easier and less stressful to be unethical (if you're not caught) versus actively combatting unethical activities, especially if an executive is involved with an issue or a situation.

In far too many of my professional experiences, I worked with and witnessed individuals who had a desire to "win or succeed at any cost." This desire for success was pursued without any concerns about the collateral damage that led to individuals being unnecessarily disrespected, retaliated against, and treated like trash. For me, I never understood this mentality, as I was taught to treat everyone (from the president to the janitor) the same because everyone should be treated with dignity and respect. Unfortunately, this belief isn't always shared or given in return.

For example, while contracting for several organizations (including a government agency) that used many consulting companies, these organizations had competitive environments in which resources would purposely not disclose information, criticize the other contract resources work to obtain more positions, delay the completion of project deliverables, or use other tactics with a goal of positioning their consulting companies for additional work.

At other times, I witnessed and experienced workplace bullying, verbal assaults, and physical attacks that were intentionally done to attempt to dominate or intimidate.

In other situations, I worked for executives who would give the appearance of ethical behavior. However, if the company's revenue was in jeopardy, the executives would instruct employees to do whatever it took to obtain or maintain revenue, including making questionable changes to reports to better its position.

It's important to note that all money isn't good, but honestly earned money is always satisfying.

Furthermore, companies shouldn't be reactive in addressing ethical compliance issues. Instead, companies should be proactive via reviews of its operations to identify any potential issues. Also, companies should support and encourage its employees to report any potential or actual questionable or unethical activities, along with monitoring any employee who reports any potential unethical activities to protect them from any type of retaliation.

Reinforcing ethical activities isn't something that's performed once and forgotten until the next review cycle, because ethical operational models must be integrated into an organization's culture. Therefore, ethical training must be conducted at a minimum of once a year. Moreover, executive leadership must visibly reinforce and display acceptable ethical activities throughout the year, as an organization's ethical role models.

Executive management's conduct is very important because company resources (e.g., employees, temporary personnel) will evaluate their activities as a litmus test to determine and gauge whether their activities are appropriate. If management doesn't act and/or behave ethically, then it can be very difficult for a company to develop and enforce an ethical culture.

It's interesting that many societies put an emphasis on individuals doing the right thing(s). Although, ethical activities aren't highlighted often enough and not always wanted or appreciated. For example, news reports about ethical activities focus primarily on those who did something unethical. Seldom do reports highlight individuals who are exemplary role models. If ethical behavior is desired, then there should be more coverage about individuals who encountered ethical dilemmas and choose to act and/or behave ethically. Also, it would be useful to spotlight individuals (even if not by name) who report questionable or unethical activities.

If ethical activities are wanted, perhaps there should be more examples highlighted to reinforce the desired activities.

Ethical activities shouldn't be done just because someone is watching, or to achieve a personal motive. Ethics are about purposely acting and/or behaving in a manner that doesn't use individuals, systems, processes, information, etc. to achieve questionable or unethical goals and objectives.

Ethical behavior is about conducting yourself in ways that are open, honest, and without any intent to achieve something fraudulently, even if others choose to behave unethically.

Nobody is perfect and most individuals have had a moment

that wasn't their finest, even me as the author of this book. However, a bad choice at a single moment in time isn't necessarily an intent to engage in unethical activities in the future.

Questionable acts and behaviors should be used as teachable moments to help direct individuals toward activities that align with acceptable and expected standards of ethical behavior.

Many times, unethical situations occur because there's an opportunity to engage in inappropriate activities due to a lack of controls, wrongful thoughts about a situation, or other factors. Furthermore, individuals will sometimes consider the costs or consequences of getting caught engaging in unethical activities instead of reflecting on making appropriate ethical decisions.

Regardless of the implementation of proper controls, some individuals will test the limits of processes and/or procedures to achieve their ulterior motives. In these situations, it can sometimes be very difficult to prevent certain activities if there's an intent to be unethical.

Everyone must make a personal choice as to whether to act and/or behave ethically. Notwithstanding, almost every person has felt pressure to do something that didn't align with their beliefs, wasn't acceptable to them, or pushed the boundaries of the intent of a policy, procedure, or a law. However, an ability to make tough decisions to be ethical despite overwhelming pressure to do otherwise are the moments that personal character is built, defined, and developed.

Oftentimes, someone's activities are related to their ideology (forced or not) and the perceived benefit(s) and risk(s) of being caught. These factors are used to determine if questionable or unethical activities will be used to achieve their goals or objectives. Therefore, perception is a significant factor in someone's desire to be ethical. Notwithstanding, a decision to act or behave ethically is always a personal choice.

These considerations are the reasons that individuals must understand and remember that: "Ethical Opportunity Cost: It's (truly) a matter of choice."

Therefore, what will you choose to do?

APPENDICES

APPENDIX A:

Ethical Behavior –
Individual Responsibility

Individuals learn about and discuss ethical behavior as a conceptual exercise. However, the number of individuals that face a significant, personal ethical dilemma may not be as large. Therefore, someone's beliefs about an action that would be taken during these exercises might not always reflect reality while faced with an ethical dilemma.

Many ethical training classes provide a description of an ethical situation, along with guidelines on ways to respond to ethical violations. Although, oftentimes, these classes don't factor into the decision-making process the reason(s) that ethical decisions should also include a consideration about personal ethics, and not business and societal ethics alone.

Some might wonder if the individual(s) that lead ethical discussions would follow the desired behavior espoused. Unfortunately, the answer isn't always "yes", as there are well documented cases of individuals that were supposed to lead by example but instead used their power or influence to achieve personal gains.

Another consideration is related to someone's analysis as to whether a behavior reached a level of a punishable offense, which can be a major factor with unethical behavior or enforcement. Therefore, one of the biggest challenges with ethical compliance is related to the individual(s) authorized to be the enforcer(s).

Consistent ethical enforcement is critical, as it provides an example of punishable behavior and is a deterrent for unethical actions or behaviors. However, enforcement isn't always possible. Sometimes a decision is made within policy guidelines, but the decision stretches the policy's intent. This can be especially true if a decision to be unethical benefits an external stakeholder or a decision doesn't hurt the company the individual is supposed to protect (e.g., directing work primarily to a friend's consulting company). In this illustration, business ethical standards may not be violated per se. However, the actions of the decision maker(s) are extremely questionable.

Enforcement isn't the biggest factor with ethical compliance. The major factors related to compliance are individual character and intent, as the application of ethical behavior is ultimately a personal choice.

For example, in December 2011, Mitch Gilbert found two unmarked Caesars Palace envelopes that contained $10K in cash[10]. Mr. Gilbert actively searched and ultimately returned the money to a grateful individual (Ignacio Marquez) who lost the envelopes while running to catch a flight. In this scenario, Mr. Gilbert's personal ethics led to the correct decision to return the money to the owner. The outcome of Mr. Gilbert's decision will have a greater impact due to the illustration of outstanding character to his children. It's also an example of superior morals for all who learn about Mr. Gilbert's extremely ethical behavior. This is a very good demonstration of personal ethics.

A business example of ethical behavior is related to an employee working on a contract for a state governmental agency ("agency"). In this example, an agency's representative requested that the audit results be changed to support its budgetary, strategic, and political needs.

---

[10] "Traveler Returns $10K in Lost Gambling Earnings", CNN.com, CNN Wire Staff: http://www.cnn.com/2011/12/27/us/colorado-money-returned; retrieved 9/19/13.

The issue with this request is that the audit findings didn't reflect the requested changes. The employee presented the agency's demand to the company's executive team. The executive team initially agreed that the requested changes shouldn't be made. However, after the agency threatened to put the company into default if the changes weren't made as requested, the company instructed the employee to change the results to reflect the agency's wishes. The executives' directions to alter the audit results (to reflect the agency's needs instead of the results) were refused by the employee. Then, the employee chose to resign instead of making the changes because the employee considered the requests to be unethical, along with being against their ethics, morals, character, and values.

Someone with a motivation to be deceptive or unethical will do so regardless of the potential to be caught, the immediate impact, or the long-term consequences of their decision. Conversely, an ethical person might or might not act based on a business' operating practices but will customarily respond accordingly based on their moral and ethical beliefs.

Ethical training should teach individuals to not abdicate personal responsibilities to make honest, ethical decisions that may be unpopular. The fortitude to stand-alone and make a difficult ethical decision (and not engage in inappropriate behavior (e.g., for money, job security, other factors)) takes guts and courage. This moral fortitude will ultimately be rewarded as a "strength of character" that is beyond reproach.

Ethical training must emphasize the importance of individual responsibility to make an appropriate, honest, and ethical decision. Otherwise, ethical dilemmas may be determined by social or office norms instead of someone's ethical consideration.

Ethics training must continue to detail company policy but should also stress individual responsibility and decision-making to resist any direction(s) to engage in questionable or inappropriate behavior (even from a senior leader). Otherwise, ethical dilemmas might be determined by inappropriate factors instead of a decision being made based on appropriate, honest, and ethical behavior.

APPENDIX B:

Are You Really

Committed to Your Beliefs?

Imagine that someone found a bag which contained $100,000. Might the money be returned; would the person keep it? In response to these questions, many individuals will most likely proclaim that there would be an attempt to return the money to its rightful owner. However, what if someone's circumstances are challenging and the person doesn't have any hope[11]? Then, might individuals behave differently than expected during challenging times? The answers to these questions are more complicated than one might think.

Challenging times can cause individuals to perform self-analysis to determine who the person really is at that moment and in the world. Furthermore, anytime someone's actions, situations, or beliefs are challenged, these are the moments that often lead to individuals beginning to move past their everyday existence, while also questioning the foundation for their beliefs.

It's easy to communicate to others and yourself the things that might be done in the future. However, given individual circumstances, situations, opportunities, or motives, as someone's beliefs don't always translate into their thoughts, actions, or behaviors.

Beliefs don't always reflect someone's thoughts, actions, or behaviors because beliefs can be influenced based on a/an:

- Self-Interest – action taken to meet someone's personal needs or objectives

---

[11] Reference the article "What If?!" in Appendix E.

- Impact to Others – a realization that someone's views impact others' rights, happiness, or pursuits

- Influence (e.g., peers, family, friends) – others' input (positive or negative) can cause someone to align with a different position

- Politics – an attempt to influence others to achieve someone's motive(s) or hidden agenda(s)

- Situation – something happens that is so significant that it causes a change (temporary or long-term) in someone's position

There are numerous examples of individuals who proclaim their belief(s) and then conveniently change their position(s) due to situations or circumstances within their own circle-of-influence.

For example:

- Executives initially refuse to do something questionable for a client and then does it anyway after the client threatens the loss of future business

- A manager who doesn't protect an employee from workplace abuse and then feels differently after similar behavior happens to them

- Senator Rob Portman's changed position on gay marriage after his son revealed that he's gay

Many times, individual beliefs are a concept, consideration, or a convenience[12] versus being something that someone believes, will defend, and acts upon. Although, challenging moments, times, and situations can (and sometimes do) force individuals to question or redefine their belief system(s) to align with other factors or considerations.

Individuals must use their core beliefs as a foundation for their actions, behaviors, and choices. Otherwise, beliefs that aren't well-defined and solidified shouldn't be the basis for someone's reflections or a representation of their true self. The significance of this point is that someone's character is driven by their beliefs, which are demonstrated by their thoughts, actions, or behaviors over time and not a single moment in time.

---

[12] Reference the article "Belief: An Underutilized Tool" in Appendix C to review definitions for concept, consideration, or convenience, as it relates to the topic of belief.

APPENDIX C:

Belief –

An Underutilized Tool

There are many life lessons taught every day, such as ways to deal with others, subject matter expertise, and learning basic survival skills. However, there isn't enough time allocated to teach individuals about the power of belief. This is surprising because belief is often a cornerstone of success. Moreover, if individuals don't believe in themselves, then the reason that others should believe in their activities or causes might not be as great.

Belief is a thought, feeling, or an internal drive that can be used to overcome an obstacle, advance toward a goal, or move beyond past challenges… sometimes despite overwhelming odds. Belief isn't required to move forward. Although, it's an important tool to help summon the energy to persevere during difficult moments or challenging times. Furthermore, the biggest benefit of possessing belief is that it supports something that is significant to someone, even if nobody else agrees with it.

Belief is something that is true to an individual, very personal, needs to be developed, and can be a powerful tool for personal development. It's also a characteristic that can help individuals move forward, solve an issue, or to achieve a goal. Nevertheless, everyone doesn't have belief in themselves or may choose not to leverage their belief system to maximize their potential. Some reasons that belief might not be fully utilized are self-doubt, fear, or others' opinions. Notwithstanding, a significant reason that belief isn't used more often is that life experiences greatly influence an individual's ability to believe.

Things that happen during someone's lifetime effect their perspective and outlook. If an individual has had positive experiences associated with their beliefs, then their outlook is usually more positive. Conversely, if an individual has had bad experiences associated with their beliefs, then their outlook might be more negative. Although, a single bad experience won't always impact someone's outlook, unless an individual learns to SEE; that is, the individual experiences a (S)ignificant (E)motional (E)vent.

Once an individual begins to SEE, there is a realization (temporary or long-term) that something that was once believed to be unimportant is actually important or something that was believed to be important might not be as significant.

There are several components of belief:

- Concept – someone envisions a way to accomplish a task, activity, or project, which doesn't need to be fully understood for an idea to be developed

- Consideration – something is evaluated as a possibility, but hasn't been selected as a viable option

- Convenience – something that is used, done, or believed only if there's a potential benefit to someone's position, situation, or desired outcome

Oftentimes, belief might not be used sufficiently because of a lack of confidence, questionable arrogance, or a negative roadblock. Therefore, belief must be developed and maintained to achieve an internal balance that will support their goals, which includes an ability to be positive in their actions, to not be confident in a condescending manner, and to prevent any self-defeating activities that might prevent themselves or others from making forward-progress.

Belief can be a challenge because no matter the amount that someone wants something to be true. There aren't any guarantees that a belief is correct, achievable, plausible, possible, reasonable, or viable. As a result, belief requires faith in something that (many times) cannot be proven to be achievable or attainable at the time it's pursued.

Other challenges with the development of belief are that individuals:

- have doubts
- don't have others' support
- aren't confident in their own capabilities
- have a need for approval
- haven't solidified their belief
- have a fear that prevents a pursuit of something that might be true

Belief helps to provide energy to complete something that someone wants to achieve. However, anyone who doesn't believe in something that is thought, done, or pursued can give-up long before the desired outcome is achieved. For this reason, individuals must understand that belief isn't required to accomplish something; although, belief can be a significant factor between experiencing success or failure.

Activities that can help develop belief:

- Work on a dream despite fears, which sometimes requires moving past personal limitations and barriers to develop an idea or to achieve a desired outcome.

- Consider an idea to be in-progress and build on it.

- Act as if there isn't a possibility of failure.

- Continue to be self-motivated, even if there are setbacks.

- Minimize doubts and worries to maximize opportunities for success.

- Learn a lot from each effort, even if the outcome isn't as desired or expected.

Beliefs might not always be realized. However, individuals who don't pursue positive beliefs can limit their opportunities and options, along with minimizing their possibilities for a better future for themselves and others.

Remember… no matter the length of your journey, always be your best.

Additional information on the development of belief can be obtained in Dr. Young's solution-oriented book Management Spotlight: Belief.

APPENDIX D:

Are You Really

Who You Think You Are?

Individuals often rush through the world to complete activities each day to get through their daily lives; many times, running so fast that there isn't sufficient time to slow down and ask: Who am I; what am I doing; am I really who I think I am?

The last question "Am I really who I think I am?" is a question that I never thought I would ask myself. However, once some impactful moments arrived, I was forced to ask myself the other questions: Who am I; what am I doing?

It's sometimes said that opportunities are missed because someone isn't actively looking for something that's wanted. Although, if an unexpected event, choice, or outcome occurs, these moments can sometimes force an individual to stop, take notice, and sometimes change direction. It's in these moments that an individual often learns to SEE; that is, an individual experiences a (S)ignificant (E)motional (E)vent that forces a self-examination of their own reality. Then, after experiencing growth by learning to SEE, individuals sometimes begin to ask themselves tough questions about the things that are or aren't believed to be.

These reflective questions (related to an individual's decision making) are based on three perspectives:

- Mental – decisions made based on thoughts about the elements under evaluation, such as the factors of, the considerations about, and the impact of an individual's choices. These decisions can be more difficult due to over-thinking, analyzing too much, or being convinced to believe something that isn't in alignment with an individual's beliefs

- Emotional – choices made based on an affecting response can cause a decision to be adversely impacted due to heightened sensory stimulation. These decisions can challenge an individual's ability to distance their feelings from external stimuli

- Spiritual – the mental and emotional perspectives can cause an individual to toil over their life's direction, because an individual's activities normally reflect their spirit and core beliefs. Moreover, an individual's core beliefs are often used to minimize opportunities for their mental or emotional perspectives from unnecessarily overriding their values

Any individual who uses the convenience of a situation to justify any action and/or behavior that doesn't align with their supposed core beliefs must question the conviction of their beliefs… as core beliefs aren't situational. However, there may be times that an individual's core beliefs are redefined based on new discoveries, corrections to previous opinions, or purposeful decisions to change their viewpoints. Despite these potential adjustments, core beliefs aren't as fluid as opinions which can change rapidly from one moment to the next.

In training for my professional career, there was never a conversation or a consideration about the possibility that I might need to make decisions that would cause me to choose between standing firm in my beliefs or being a party (willing or not) to questionable and/or unethical activities. Furthermore, none of my extensive training prepared me for the heart-wrenching decisions that were required to choose between remaining at a job and a conflict with my core beliefs that might impact my earning potential.

The easiest thing to do while faced with moral, ethical, spiritual, or other challenges is to ignore the activities of others and convince yourself that others' questionable and/or unethical activities aren't any of your concern.

During the times I encountered these types of situations, these incidents made me question myself and my beliefs. Specifically, are my beliefs really true to me; are my beliefs situational in nature; are my beliefs[13] reflective of who I am or who I want to be? The answer I sought was in this last question.

By making tough decisions during challenging times these circumstances made me truly examine not just the example I set externally, but also the standard that I set for myself internally. The external example is easy to fake and often individuals do to appease others, to cover their actions, or to receive a personal benefit… even though I didn't in these situations.

The internal example isn't as easy to fake, move past, or convince yourself that it's actually true. Unlike the external projection, the internal projection might be personally impactful long after a current situation. Therefore, will you act and/or behave a certain way for others, but then continue to toil over some of the worst disappointment possible… to yourself?

Some of the hardest things that an individual can do during their lifetime are to live with the outcome of their actions, behaviors, choices, or decisions. For this reason, does it not make sense that an individual ensures that their spiritual, emotional, and mental perspectives/decisions are aligned?

---

[13] Reference this article in Appendix C: Belief – An Underutilized Tool.

The answer to this last question isn't for me to provide for others; however, my hope is that this question is something individuals will thoughtfully consider.

Additional information on the development of belief can be obtained in Dr. Young's solution-oriented book Management Spotlight: Belief.

APPENDIX E:

What If?!

What if a decision you were afraid to, chose not to, or didn't make could've changed your life and others? This might seem to be an unanswerable question but consider another. What if you didn't act, decide, or respond because you allowed someone's considerations to stop you from doing the right thing or pursing your dream(s); were directed away from doing something that might help you to achieve your potential; caused you to doubt yourself due to their questions about your abilities or capabilities? These types of reflective questions can lead individuals to later think... "What if?!"

"What if?!" is a question asked by many throughout their lives, but the worst time to consider it is on your deathbed. Too many individuals, don't achieve their potential simply due to fear (e.g., taking a chance/step, others' opinions, failing). A video[14] about individuals not living up to their potential captures this best, along with adding that dreams sometimes die forever because the individual who could have given them life didn't pursue them.

In Jim Carey's commencement address[15] at the 2014 Maharishi University of Management's graduation, he shared that his father didn't believe it was possible for him to be a successful comedian... so he didn't pursue it. Instead, he accepted a safe job as an accountant, but was let go from this job; subsequently, his family struggled to survive. During this speech Mr. Carey said, "So many of us choose our paths out of fear disguised as practicality." He went on to say, "I learned many great lessons from my father. Not the least of which is that you can fail at

---

[14] Motivational Video: Live Your Life Over: youtu.be/jFunNbeIzRk

[15] Jim Carey's commencement address: youtu.be/V80-gPkpH6M?t=610 (watch from 10:10 - 11:46)

what you don't want, so you might as well take a chance at doing what you love."

"What if?!" the direction of your life or your life's purpose wasn't driven by the decisions that you made, but instead by the ones you tormented over and didn't make? Could these moments of indecision (if addressed directly) have been the catalyst that pushed you toward a direction that otherwise you might not have gone? These tough moments or questions might be presented as a crossroad to determine if someone is ready to live a life that wasn't or couldn't be imaged as a possibility.

These types of internal dilemmas and conflicts I know very well. During difficult and critical moments in my life, I questioned my beliefs to determine if the things I said and did were really true to me. At times, someone will proclaim to have strong beliefs about something until the person is able to actually make a choice or decision. Then, once confronted or forced to make a choice, these same individuals will back away from, question, or attack their own position.

During challenging years, I made difficult choices due to conflicts between my beliefs and my willingness to be complicit to others' unethical activities. These gut-wrenching choices led to unimaginable tough times that had me within moments of taking my life, but at the same time these visceral moments caused me to grow the most emotionally, mentally, and spiritually. Moreover, I learned that my choices reflect my commitment to who I am and who I want to be, but are also driven by my desire to not want to later ask myself:

What if I hadn't done the right thing and chose to ignore or went along with questionable / unethical / illegal activities for the sake of maintaining my job and financial standing by sacrificing my principles?

By "Choosing To Take A Stand" against actions and behaviors I knew weren't right, I began to redefine and transform myself into unexpectedly the better man I am today. These types of tough moments (for example: failure, disappointment, and loss) are sometimes the biggest factors and impetus for growth and enlightenment. I could have played it safe (like Jim Carey's father) and made a very good salary for myself, but I wouldn't have been true to myself, my beliefs, or also self-fulfilled. The amazing thing that happened during my darkest days was that I really got to learn about who I am, which I didn't do before... and maybe in some ways was afraid to do. Today I can honestly and confidently look at myself in the mirror and say, "I know who I am!," which is a priceless feeling.

Frederick Nietzsche's quote, "He who has a why to live can bear almost any how." has significant meaning for my life. If it wasn't for my ability to determine my "why" during the tumultuous years, I wouldn't have been able to handle my "how." This would have also prevented me from discovering my passion, purpose, and ability to maximize my personal value, which is simply to help and teach others.

> Note: By addressing my life's challenges directly, I unleased and gave myself permission to: create an educational nonprofit that teaches inmates about life, business, and soft skills; become an inspirational speaker who discusses overcoming challenges; helped depressed individuals and those who lost loved ones to death-by-

suicide to better understand this mental health challenge, educated individuals about workplace bullying; connected with thousands around the world through my writing; learned to live my life on purpose.

The easiest thing to do during tough times is to have a negative perspective, engage in destructive behavior, or sometimes just quit trying. However, this type of defeatist attitude won't help you to do something that matters for yourself... and others. While confronted with difficult choices that have a potential to effect my future (and sometimes others), I found solace in one of my quotes from Part III in my "It's a Crazy World... Learn From It" series (p. 20):

> *Many individuals are afraid of jail; however, they often lock themselves in their own prisons. Be your own warden and set yourself free of unnecessary worry, doubts, fears, and perceived limitations.*

The tough lessons I've learned is that beliefs[16] aren't always as firm as some might think. Too often, individuals proclaim to have a belief (something generally believed to be true), but many times it's simply a consideration (something true for that person) that might change under certain criteria. Although, many actions are based on convenience (a moment exception depending on circumstances), instead of a personal belief[17] or consideration.

---

[16] Reference the article "Belief: An Underutilized Tool" in Appendix C.

[17] This video "Belief: A Powerful Component of Success (youtu.be/ftAbx0oxndU)" was recorded one week and one day after I almost died-by-suicide. I presented to an audience, but I was attempting to convince myself to "believe" again.

Individuals can miss opportunities because there isn't a belief that something is possible, their considerations aren't enough to drive their desire(s)/determination to act, or it isn't convenient for someone to persevere to summon their internal strength to move forward despite (sometimes overwhelming) obstacles.

There are so many "What if?!" questions that go unanswered due to fear but imagine the potential impact of pushing yourself to make a tough choice that could positively change your life or others. Might your actions or behaviors be different during challenging moments? Perhaps... Unfortunately, unless individuals make active choices to "What if?!" questions, the outcome of these missed opportunities or decisions might not ever be known.

Instead of wondering right now... "What if the writer of the piece is correct?" ... create a list of "What if?!" questions for yourself and answer them. By actively choosing and proactively planning to make decisions about your life, you'll never have to wonder... "What if?!"

APPENDIX F:

Confronted with an Ethical Dilemma:

What Will You Do?

It's easier to speculate about something that might be done in the future than to act, especially if it's a difficult decision that has personal implications or direct impacts. This type of mental positioning can often be shortsighted, misguided, and self-serving if there aren't full considerations (versus a cursory review) about potential outcomes that might occur due to a failure to prevent wrongful activities. Notwithstanding, one of the biggest factors in ethical decision-making is personal beliefs, which aren't always fully considered, evaluated, or processed.

Beliefs aren't always considered while making decisions. Nevertheless, personal beliefs effect the way someone processes a situation, considers options, or acts. During an ethical evaluation, beliefs represent a culmination of direct and indirect experiences throughout someone's life. If someone is unethical (even a little bit), then this behavior can negatively impact their future ethical decision-making. The rationale for this is that once someone acts or behaves inappropriately, then it can be easier to do it again. Moreover, if someone's morals and values direct them to behave in a certain way and then the person acts differently depending on the situation, then what might this suggest about their character?! The answer to this question isn't simple because a bad choice at a moment doesn't mean that someone will make the same type of decision again.

Generally, the manner in which someone makes a decision is more complicated than a "yes or no" response. Arguably, the greater the potential for personal gain(s) or negative impact(s), the more likely it can be for someone to make a decision that's more aligned with punitive avoidance.

Beliefs and decision-making are collectively driven by three components:

- Concept - something that's generally accepted to be true
  - Is this considered to be true?
- Consideration - a determination as to whether something is true for an individual
  - Is this true for me?
- Convenience - a decision made for personal risk reduction, benefit, or gain
  - Is this true for me at this moment?

Ethical decision-making goes beyond the often used and limited evaluation as to whether something is "good or bad" or "right or wrong." Therefore, these three components drive individuals to test their considerations to determine if their choices and subsequent decisions are made for convenience reasons. The challenge is that tough or heart-wrenching decisions can cause individuals to analyze too much or be paralyzed by perceived personal risk(s) of making an ethical decision. However, the focus should be on understanding the value of doing the right thing(s). If the former criterion is used, then (too many times) those who engage in questionable and/or unethical behavior are (unfortunately) allowed to continue their actions. These types of inappropriate behavior are usually caused by someone's unnecessary complicity due to inaction. Consequently, anyone involved in malfeasance subsequently receives implicit approval to prolong their self-serving actions.

Individuals might not prevent questionable and/or unethical activities/behaviors due to:

- the potential impact to personal earnings
- an inability to take care of family
- the fear of retaliation
- the potential of lost opportunities
- the perceptions of others
- learned behavior that those who speak-up are harassed, punished, scrutinized, forced to resign, or terminated
- undocumented or misunderstood processes
- a mistaken belief that it's none of their business
- a lack of safeguards to protect those who report wrongdoings

Individuals usually know if their or others' behaviors are questionable or unethical. Nevertheless, ethical decisions sometimes require additional information to fully consider a situation or make a subsequent choice. The challenge (at times) can be associated with incidents that fall within an uncertain classification or someone's determination as to whether to get involved. During these types of considerations, there can be significant internal conflicts to contend with while attempting to act or behave ethically.

Choosing to take a stand against questionable or unethical activities isn't always easy. However, it's better than at best being complicit or worse being an accomplice to activities that can have negative impacts to individuals, teams, organizations, companies, and societies. Moreover, there must be societal support, training reinforcement, corporate policies, and laws to ensure that those who report illicit activities are protected. Consequently, there will be reduced misgivings about reporting those who breach their personal, fiduciary, and societal responsibilities.

Without prudent leadership and strength of character, the answer to the question "Confronted with an Ethical Dilemma: What will you do?!" will unfortunately and unnecessarily (too often) be silenced due to practices of convenience versus having the fortitude to do the right thing(s).

APPENDIX G:

Ethics Training Is Missing
the Mark: Here's Why

Ethics is a topic that's often discussed by parents, schools, organizations, and employers. These discussions usually teach individuals about the importance of being ethical: what does it mean; why is it important; what are the costs of unethical activities? This subject matter must be taught; however, the toughest parts of being ethical are almost never discussed. That is... what are the emotional, physiological, and moral challenges that individuals who don't want to be complicit to unethical behavior experience?

Before exploring the affects and effects of wanting to be ethical, the reason that ethics is important must be reviewed.

Ethics are behavioral standards that individuals, organizations, and societies apply and generally adhere to as acceptable. Without ethical standards, there can be numerous variables used to determine if something is right or wrong, good or bad. Notwithstanding these random variables, there are always individual considerations based on experiential learning; however, an individual's ethical standards are normally defined and developed by family, religious beliefs, friends, and societal practices. These standards provide common operating practices that are used to define the limits of acceptable behavior.

Generally, individuals know whether something is right or wrong. Although, there are times that ethical decisions will require additional consideration, input, or sometimes assistance to make the appropriate choice. The challenge (many times) is whenever a decision is within an unclear range, or the biggest test is making a decision about whether to get involved to resolve a known ethical issue. During these times, individuals can experience an internal battle while attempting to make an ethical decision.

The internal impacts of making tough ethical choices can impact individuals:

- Emotionally – a feeling related to a particular situation, event, or consideration

- Physiologically - a body's reaction to making a tough decision, which could be stress, anxiety, sweat, depression, etc.

- Morally - a challenge to an individual's belief system weighed against the things an individual believes to be true but may be altered while making a tough decision

These internal impacts are seldom (if ever) discussed during ethics training. This omission is unfortunate because an ability to process these intangible elements is an important factor while individuals determine whether to be ethical during certain moments.

In a time that winning at almost any cost is more pervasive, there must be an increased focus given to educating individuals about the significance of internal processing in ethical decision making (beyond the mental processing). Otherwise, a larger number of individuals are more likely to bend the limits of standards, rules, policies, or laws to receive an unfair or personal advantage.

After the allegations of ball deflation[18] by the New England Patriots prior to Super Bowl XLIX, my nephew and I discussed the potential ethical issues. During our conversation, my nephew made a couple of points to support his argument: 1) the deflation was found in the first half but didn't impact the game's outcome and 2) everyone cheats at some point. What?!

<u>The rationale used in his positioning is troubling for several reasons:</u>

- First, a determination of whether something is ethical should never be decided based on an outcome, but instead by an evaluation of a consideration, situation, or an event

- Second, a choice to be unethical cannot be validated based on attempting to justify the behavior by rationalizing the actions or activities of another

- Third, individuals must be accountable and responsible for their actions, including complicit acceptance of wrongdoings by allowing known unethical behavior (by others) to continue unchallenged

There is a cost to individuals, organizations, and societies if unethical activities aren't resolved in a timely manner. However, there are also costs to individuals' emotional, physiological, and moral health while making a choice whether to get involved with the prevention of unethical behavior.

---

[18] Young, S. L. (1/23/15). Patriots Win the Game, But Fail to Score Points With Public Opinion. Retrieved 5/20/14 from slyoung.com/patriots-ballgate.

Decisions individuals make cannot be necessarily managed by external factors. Although, if ethical training helps individuals to understand and prepare for the internal factors that might be experienced while dealing with ethical dilemmas, then more individuals will be better prepared to handle the internal impacts that can be experienced while attempting to behave ethically.

APPENDIX H:

High School Friends, Different Ethical Paths, Almost Identical Tragic Endings

This month (March) is National Ethics Awareness Month, which represents an additional opportunity to focus on and discuss ethical behavior. This topic is especially important to me as someone who took a stand against unethical behavior in several organizations, even though my ethical behavior unbelievably led to inconceivable personal costs. Regardless of the anguish experienced, I would do the same things again today. My strong belief is that a choice to remain silent about or be complicit to wrongdoings (regardless of the potential consequences) is never an acceptable option.

The following characterizes the impact of ethical choices (good and bad) on the lives of two high school friends that led to considerable turmoil for both of their lives. One would be dead months after being terminated by their employer after alleged discrepancies in expense reimbursement requests were discovered. In public records, the company terminating their employment communicated that the expenses weren't properly reimbursable or were reimbursements requested that were more than the amounts actually spent. The other individual would be moments from death-by-suicide after being negatively impacted due to making several difficult choices to not participate or be complicit to unethical behavior, including workplace bullying. These experiences are shared to highlight the issues, impacts, and devastation that can result for anyone who faces or confronts ethical dilemmas (created by themselves or forced upon them by others).

During high school these friends had a lot of good times together but were on different paths. One excelled and was academically inclined; the other was mischievous and not academically focused. Even though they took different educational and career paths, both had ambitious dreams. A while after high school, these friends didn't reconnect until a coincidental meeting at a university. At this point, one friend was driven to become a corporate mogul while the other struggled to connect with their academic pursuits. Regardless of these differences, both of their academic and professional ambitions drove them to achieve future successes.

Years later their paths crossed again. Up until this time, both achieved numerous academic, professional, and personal successes; although, their lives and pursuits continued to be vastly different. One of them achieved the prestige of becoming a financial broker and living a flashy New York lifestyle of the rich and famous, which many individuals desire. The other one struggled to rebuild their life after voluntarily leaving successful careers in organizations that had cultures, values, and authority figures who were unethical and desired to win at any cost. These beliefs and highly questionable efforts to achieve success didn't align with their concepts of ethical behavior or decent treatment of people.

Ethics is something that's stressed throughout many people's lives by their families/friends, churches, schools, organizations, and employers. It's something that's communicated as being responsible and valuable; however, the personal and sometimes professional costs to achieve and maintain ethical standards aren't always considered worth it. It's this kind of carefree mentality that results in too many incidents of purposeful, known, and ignored ethical violations. This type of conduct is too often permitted due to those who choose to be involved, are intimidated into silence, or determine the potential costs of involvement aren't worth it. The challenge is that complicit behavior (direct or indirect) is driven by a fear of getting involved, retaliation, or being labeled a snitch, which can prevent mindful actions that could stop wrongdoings, prevent a recurrence, and sometimes save lives if reported (even anonymously).

One of the biggest issues with ethical compliance is the presence of opportunity. The implementation of policies and procedures is a good starting point, but neither of these administrative items will prevent ethical misdoings without having ongoing independent processes and procedural reviews. Another preventative action to minimize the chances of administrative cover-up is to rotate individuals who are responsible for significant processes, financial, operational, or audit controls. By periodically shifting individual and/or organizational responsibilities, there are reduced opportunities to manipulate controls due to certain individuals using their insider knowledge for deceptive purposes.

There are various reasons for ethical violations, such as greed, power, intimidation/workplace bullying, personal challenges, retaliation, or other factors. These plentiful motivators can't always be identified until after the fact; nevertheless, there must be proactive and reactive mechanisms to quickly resolve any challenges prior to the emergence of bigger and more pervasive issues.

Ethical and unethical behavior can have negative costs and outcomes. While thinking about unethical behavior, individuals usually and easily understand the impacts, such as damaged reputations, broken friendships, lost jobs, public scrutiny, emotional damage, depression, and death. Conversely, individuals don't often consider or can't imagine the negative impacts of ethical behavior, which interestingly can have similar consequences.

Ethical decision making is ultimately a personal choice; although, environmental influences (e.g., friends/family, religious institutions, organizations, cultures) can impact someone's willingness, desires, and actions. However, a decision to engage in unethical behavior is still an individual activity. Everyone should remember that ethical behavior is pretty clear; the part that's gray is individual interpretation. Moreover, it's almost always better to review an earlier situation longing for a better outcome than to reflect on past actions with regret. The reason(s) someone chooses to be unethical covers a large spectrum, but many times it's tied to greed, self-esteem issues, and a desire to live beyond someone's means without honestly earning it. Notwithstanding, ethical behavior is a choice, an individual responsibility, and a reflection of the way someone wants to live their life.

My high school friend's reasons for choosing to be unethical might not ever be known. However, based on their various communications and Facebook messages prior to their death, there appeared to be a strong desire to project an image of status and extreme success. The unfortunate thing that many individuals (like my friend) realize too late is that material possessions are only a reflection of someone's financial status but cannot and will not reflect anyone's intrinsic worth. For my choices to be ethical and behave ethically, I lost a lot personally, professional, and financially… including almost losing my life. Even though my experiences as a result were an arduous journey, I still have a strong belief and desire to do the right things regardless of any potential consequences (although I occasionally make bad choices). Despite all the devastatingly painful moments I experienced, I'm a better, more focused, socially conscientious, and driven man because of it.

Challenging moments and tough decisions are part of the human experience but choosing to be unethical or being complicit to unethical behavior isn't a winning solution. Short-term gains can be achieved by and through unethical acts, but… are the long-term consequences (direct/indirect) for yourself and others worth it? In the case of my high school friend, it appears that their unethical choices and behaviors led to the loss of a life. As for me, the tough decisions I made led to reclaiming mine, along with validating to myself and others that I am the man I say I am. The value, freedom, and confidence of this last consideration is absolutely and ethically priceless!

APPENDIX I:

Becoming a Better Man

In 2014, I called one of my brothers to ask a very important question, "If anything happens to me, will you take care of ma?" My goal was to obtain confirmation for my question and then end my life, but it didn't go as planned. I began to cry, my brother started to ask questions, and then I abruptly hung-up the phone. Then, over the next hour, my brother franticly called to attempt to contact and help me.

On that cold March morning, I almost died-by-suicide because I falsely believed that I didn't have any value, and no one wanted the things I did. Also, I thought, "If being ethical caused this much pain and torment, then... why would I want to live anymore?! Even though I was ready and prepared to end my life, I didn't want to die. However, I desperately wanted the emotional pain to end with the quickest path to relief.

Over a few years in different organizations, I fought against being complicit to unethical activities. The requests and directions I received (as a consultant) were surprising and shocking. In over a decade of working at Fortune 500 companies (while managing multi-million dollar projects), I was almost never asked to do anything I believed to be ethically and/or morally wrong. Notwithstanding, I did witness bad decision-making. Although, this isn't the same as intentional actions for personal gain.

At one company, after delivering independent audit results for a state government client, I was asked to change information in a report to justify an organization's desire for additional funding. After discussing this request with my company's executive team, the decision made was that the report wouldn't be changed. Then, the client threatened to no longer do business with this small consulting company if the report didn't reflect its wishes.   Shortly thereafter, my leadership team directed me to alter the report to meet the client's needs, which I refused to do because the changes didn't reflect my documented findings.

In another organization, I contracted for a federal government client. Every day I requested work to do, but I wasn't assigned any tasks to complete. My requests continued for weeks (while being paid to sit at my desk) until I was finally directed to develop a project budget. Upon requesting verifiable budget information from the project's executive, I was directed to enter whatever costs I wanted to input without any information to substantiate the forecast.   After this incident, being continuously underemployed, and being asked to engage in unethical activities, I sought other employment.

There was another incident in which I was constantly belittled, scolded, and essentially called "stupid" several times. After reporting these incidents to my executive manager, the hostile and unprovoked attacks didn't abate. As a result, I couldn't justifiably continue to work for an organization in which I was disrespected, demeaned, and devalued.

After a period of short assignments, I couldn't obtain gainful employment. As the months and years passed, my drive to succeed deteriorated, my future earning potential was highly uncertain, I lost hope, and I was extremely depressed. These pressures led to the day I almost ended my life.

The primary things that saved my life were: (1) my brother telling me, "Stacey, this is a just a moment; you need to get past this moment.", and (2) going to the Arlington County Detention Facility (ACDF) a few hours after I almost died-by-suicide to teach inmates. At the detention facility, surprisingly, I couldn't enter that day because it was on lockdown. Nevertheless, by mustering the courage to go there, I took affirmative action to begin to reclaim my life and drive my future.

The ironic thing is that teaching inmates isn't something I ever wanted to do. Yet, my friends and family convinced me to do it, along with suggesting that my inspirational books should be used with this population. Interestingly, my time at the jail teaching incarcerated individuals made me forget my personal troubles that kept me in a depressive state. Being in this environment and teaching these men gave me a renewed sense of purpose, meaningful work, and value.

I wrote this quote during my darkest days to help remind me about the importance of forward-progress:

> *Your darkest days don't define you, but instead these experiences provide opportunities for you to display your strength and character, which will ultimately drive the individual you become.*

There can be other plans for our lives that are communicated in sometimes subtle messages that can be missed if we're not open to receiving them. These messages can validate our existence, journey, and path.

During my first ACDF visit to determine if I could teach at a jail, something surprising happened. As I entered the housing unit in which I would teach, unexpectedly someone yelled my name. At first, I ignored it because I didn't know anyone at this jail. Then, I heard my name again, which was directed toward me by someone I didn't recognize. After getting my attention, I was reminded that we were friends in high school. This experience changed my perspective about teaching inmates because I connected to a common bond of humanity, reflected on the significance of this chance encounter, and accepted my outreach with humility.

Another one of my quotes that helped strengthen my will was:

> *Many individuals are afraid of jail; however, they often lock themselves in their own prisons. Be your own warden and set yourself free of unnecessary worry, doubts, fears, and perceived limitations.*

My heart-wrenching choices taught me powerful lessons about living a purposeful life:

- First, fighting to do the right things and making positive changes is always beneficial even if the short-term pain might seem unbearable

- Second, current circumstances might affect me, but it doesn't need to define my future unless I choose to unnecessarily surrender

- Third, even during the worst moments, I can support others while at the same time helping myself

- Fourth, wasting time engaging in self-deprecating behavior or destructive activities will only hurt myself while not improving my current situation

- Fifth; there's an immeasurable value in not needlessly losing yourself to conform to others' self-serving interests

I humbly learned throughout these experiences that with positive, definitive choices (while confronting unimaginable circumstances and overwhelming odds), I won't ever need to wonder if I did the right things. This mentality will allow me to intentionally create the life "I purposely choose to live."

Learn about Dr. Young's work to raise awareness about the impacts of harassment and workplace bullying: slyoung.com/workplace-bullying

Figures

<u>1.0:</u> Baseline Representation of Ethical Behavior

<u>1.1:</u> Cashier's Initial Ethical Baseline

<u>1.2:</u> Cashier's Decreasing Ethical Baseline

References

Ethics Resource Center (ERC). "National Business Ethics Survey of the U.S. Workforce" (2014). Used with permission from the Ethics Resource Center, 2345 Crystal Drive, Suite 201, Arlington, VA 22202. Online (ethics.org), Retrieved: 3/14/14.

"Traveler Returns $10K in Lost Gambling Earnings", CNN.com, CNN Wire Staff: cnn.com/2011/12/27/us/colorado-money-returned; Retrieved: 9/19/13.

Young, S. L. (12/6/13). Are You Really Committed to Your Beliefs? Retrieved 5/20/14 from slyoung.com/committed-beliefs.

Young, S. L. (5/12/14). Are You Really Who You Think You Are? Retrieved 5/20/14 from slyoung.com/who-are-you.

Young, S. L. (3/26/18). Becoming A Better Man. Retrieved 1/31/21 from slyoung.com/better-man.

Young, S. L. (12/1/13). Belief: An Underutilized Tool. Retrieved 5/20/14 from slyoung.com/belief.

Young, S. L. Bullies… They're In Your Office, Too: Could you be one? Beyond SPRH, LLC, 2013 - 2014, 2023 - 2024. Print.

Young, S. L. (10/4/16). Confronted with an Ethical Dilemma: What Will You Do? Retrieved 1/11/19 from slyoung.com/ethical-dilemma.

Young, S. L. (9/19/13). Ethical Behavior: Individual Responsibility. Retrieved 5/20/14 from slyoung.com/ethical-behavior.

Young, S. L. (2/18/15). Ethical Training is Missing the Mark: Here's Why. Retrieved 1/17/16 from slyoung.com/ethics-training.

Young, S. L. (3/25/16). High School Friends, Different Ethical Paths, Almost Identical Tragic Endings. Retrieved 1/16/21 from slyoung.com/ethical-paths.

Young, S. L. It's a Crazy World… Learn From It: Part II – Moving Forward. Beyond SPRH, LLC, 2012 - 2014, 2023 - 2024, page 34. Print.

Young, S. L. (1/23/15). Patriots Win the Game, But Fail to Score Points With Public Opinion. Retrieved 5/20/14 from slyoung.com/patriots-ballgate

Young, S. L. (9/21/15). What If?! Retrieved 1/17/16 from slyoung.com/what-if.

About the Author

Dr. S. L. Young is an author, professor, career coach, former HuffPost contributor, founder of the educational non-profit organization "Saving Our Communities at Risk Through Educational Services (SOCARTES – socartes.org)," founder of the for-profit company "Beyond SPRH, LLC – beyondsprh.com)," and former host of "Beyond Just Talk with S. L. Young." The topics of his books include belief, communication, negotiation, time management, workplace bullying, ethics, overcoming challenges, and inspirational quotes.

In 2012, Dr. Young became an author with the release of his first book in the "It's a Crazy World… Learn From It" series.

Dr. Young graduated from the American University in Washington, D.C. with a Bachelor of Science in Business Administration (BSBA) degree in International Business with a marketing concentration. He also graduated from The George Washington University in Washington, D.C. with two degrees: Master of Business Administration (MBA) in Finance and Investments with a human resources concentration and a Master of Science (M.S.) in Project Management. In 2023, at Marymount University, he successfully defended his Doctorate (Ed.D.) in Educational Leadership and Organizational Innovation. The focus of his doctoral research was "Student Engagement's Impact on Academic Performance for Nontraditional Students in a Community College Environment."

In 2022, Dr. Young was inducted into and became a life member of The Honor Society of Phi Kappa Phi. In 2023, he was inducted into The Honor Society of Kappa Delta Pi. Additionally, he's a life-member of the professional business fraternity of Alpha Kappa Psi.

Dr. Young's professional career includes approximately fifteen years with Fortune 500 companies, including Bell Atlantic, MCI, Sprint Nextel, and various consulting engagements, in the areas of billing, customer service, engineering, finance, information technology, network security, operations, product development, and software quality assurance.

Dr. Young, for nearly fifteen years, has taught a variety of classes (i.e., Introduction to Business, Entrepreneurship, Business Communication, Marketing, Small Business Management, Organizational Behavior, and Principles of Management at the Northern Virginia Community College. He has also taught at Marymount University for over three years.

In 2012, Dr. Young created SOCARTES to share life and business lessons with individuals in opportunity "at-risk" communities. Through his work with this organization, he created additional pathways for him to give-back to and make meaningful connections in various communities.

Dr. Young's passion to help others is fueled based on his abilities to excel academically and professionally. These accomplishments occurred after being directed to leave high school in tenth grade, graduating in the bottom 8% of his high school class, and leaving several colleges prior to becoming actively engaged in the process of learning. These experiences drove his desires to tirelessly help others in meaningful ways and various environments.

In January 2015, Dr. Young launched Beyond SPRH, which provides solution-oriented services to help individuals and organizations to maximize output potential.

In 2018, Dr. Young received special recognition for his work to educate an incarcerated population. The first was the Martin Luther King, Jr. Drum Major Innovative Service Award from the U.S. Department of Education for Faith-Based and Neighborhood Partnerships, in collaboration with the White House Initiative for Educational Excellence for African-Americans. The second was the Distinguished County Service Award from Volunteer Arlington (a program of the Leadership Center for Excellence).

Dr. Young is driven to share his knowledge that leads to developmental opportunities (especially for underserved and marginalized communities). Through his authentic lived-experiences overcoming challenges, Dr. Young works tirelessly to inspire others to overcome challenges and pursue their dreams, too.

Dr. Young's published works:

- Above Expectations – My Story: an unlikely journey from almost failing high school to becoming a college professor

- Bullies… They're In Your Office, Too: Could you be one?

- Choosing To Take A Stand: Changed me, my life, and my destiny

- Ethical Opportunity Cost: It's a matter of choice

- It's a Crazy World… Learn From It:

  o Part I – Taking Care of Me

  o Part II – Moving Forward

  o Part III – Keeping It Going

  o Part IV – The Journey Continues

- Management Spotlight:

  - Belief

  - Communication

  - Critical Thinking/Thick-Skin

  - Negotiation

  - Time Management

  - Workplace Bullying

- Soft Skills Development:

  - Belief

  - Communication

  - Critical Thinking/Thick-Skin

  - Negotiation

  - Time Management

- Turning Darkness Into Light: Inspiring lessons after a near-suicide

www.ingramcontent.com/pod-product-compliance
Lightning Source LLC
Chambersburg PA
CBHW051454170526
45166CB00001B/246